PRAISE FOR *BELOW THE LINE*

"If Michael Connolly were an ex-Hollywood agent who knew the cream of show biz and the sour milk of its lowlifes like he knows the back of his brass-knuckled hand, he might have created Mike Millek and his foot-to-the-floor dark ride, *Below the Line.* Set along the seams of the real movie business--as its street-savvy author Jankowski has lived and savored it--with an A-list casting call of characters so real they're scary, Mike Millek is as hardboiled as a shark in hot water and his Los Angeles is a City of Angles. So if you take your java noir with a double shot of espresso, take just one bite of *Below the Line* and it will reel you in...hook, line and sinker!"

> —Rupert Holmes, Edgar and Tony-winning author
> creator of the AMC-TV series *Remember WENN*,
> and author of *Where the Truth Lies*

"Batten down the hatches for a hard-boiled storm. *Below the Line* is an impressive debut, a suspenseful Nautical Noir on the fringe of Hollywood's dream factory. Taut, vivid tough-guy pulp in the tradition of John D. MacDonald and Mickey Spillane."

> —John Shepphird, Shamus Award-winning author

"Babes, boats and betrayal! Steve Jankowski's thrilling debut crime novel jets through the gritty sets of Hollywood to the deadly Pacific in a riveting tale worthy of Travis McGee."

> —Lawrence Maddox, author of *Fast Bang Booze*

BELOW THE LINE

STEVEN JANKOWSKI

BELOW THE LINE

DOWN&OUT
BOOKS

Down & Out Books
3959 Van Dyke Road, Suite 265
Lutz, FL 33558
DownAndOutBooks.com

Cover design by NabinKarna

ISBN: 1-64396-154-3
ISBN-13: 978-1-64396-154-5

Dedicated to memory of mentor and master storyteller, Frantisek Daniel

PROLOGUE

I was down on my hands and knees feeling around in the dark, searching for the gun. When I couldn't find it, I decided to make a run for it. I got back up to my feet and was about to run when he tackled me from behind. We rolled around in the dirt, wrestling, gouging, and trying to land punches on each other. He overpowered me as he got atop, straddling me, and got me in a chokehold. I tried to wriggle away and punch my way out of it to no use—he was not letting go. I tried prying his hands off, but they were like vices, locked in a death grip. Gasping for breath, I felt myself going. My vision was fading and as a last ditch effort I reached around, feeling the ground. I felt a good size rock, grabbed it and conjured up my last bit of strength. I crashed it into his temple with all my might, or at least what was left of it. He fell off me and I gasped for air, struggling to get to my feet. I went for the pickaxe, but he came up with the gun. He fired, hitting my hand as I reached for the handle. I spun around in pain, grabbing the pickaxe in my other hand and in a feeble attempt, threw it at him. It was enough for him to duck out of its way as I took off down the rocky, dirt hill. I heard the crack of another gunshot and felt the bullet whiz by my ear as I ran.

My bare feet were on fire as I ran and my hand was bleeding badly, but I knew I couldn't stop. I ran up to the ranger station and banged loudly on the door with my good hand. I saw a light come on inside and heard another gunshot. The bullet hit the building exploding with a loud report, splintering the wooden siding. I called out to whoever was inside to call the sheriff, and took off running again. I heard a couple more shots but kept running as fast as my bare feet could down the road.

I was all the way down near the golf course when I finally saw the deputy sheriff's car come racing up the canyon road with the lights flashing.

I ducked off the road and collapsed onto the soft fairway grass, heaving to catch my breath as the patrol car flew by. I lay in the wet grass, unable to move from pain and exhaustion. I was bleeding badly, struggling to catch my breath as my hand screamed in pain. The bullet had gone right through it between my thumb and forefinger. I held my hand to my chest, rolling in my wet T-shirt. I closed my eyes and tried to gather some strength for my next move. My torn, raw feet were burning, and the soft wet grass felt good beneath them. I wanted to get up and go but felt as if I couldn't move. I was paralyzed and just wanted to lie there and go to sleep. I knew this was not a good sign but was unable to shake it. As my breathing calmed and the adrenaline started to fade, the cool night air and dewy grass sent a shiver down my spine, jolting me back to reality. When I finally opened my eyes, he was there, standing over me with the gun pointed at my head. His face was bloodied from where I'd hit him with the rock.

"I going to fucking kill you, and then I'm going back to your boat, and I'm going to kill your fucking girlfriend."

At that moment I knew I was going to die and there wasn't a damn thing I could do about it. "Fuck you!" I said defiantly. It was all I could come up with to say.

But maybe I'm getting ahead of myself.

It all started about two weeks ago...

CHAPTER 1

There's a saying that the two best days of a boater owner's life are the day you buy your boat and the day you sell it. So here I was, hoping for best day number two, waiting for a potential buyer to show up for a test sail on my boat that I was now trying to sell. My broker, Corey, made the appointment for 2:00 p.m., and it was already twenty after. Corey was no doubt showing the potential buyer some more expensive "bikini buckets," trying to maximize his commission. My boat, a long keel, cutter-rigged ocean cruiser is not really the fashionable de rigueur of Southern California sailing that most people are looking for. It's a serious ocean cruiser for making serious voyages. It may not win many regattas, but it will get you to your distant destination in relative safety with all that Neptune throws at you. Not everyone's cup of tea for the weekend day-sailor. As I sat in the cockpit at my dock in Marina del Rey waiting, I started contemplating my life here in Southern California and how I got to where I was.

I came out to L.A. for a week and stayed for twenty-six years. So far, that is. It was one of those brutally cold winters in New York—snow, rain, sleet, and never-ending gray-sky weather that seemed to go on for months on end. I was still living in The Bronx, and I vividly remember scurrying across White Plains Road under the El train, trying to beat the traffic. I absently stomped into an ankle-deep, freezing slush-puddle in my Nike sneakers, soaking my foot. As I looked down, stamping my feet and cursing, the number 2 train roared overhead sending an icy-cold droplet down from the tracks above. It nailed me right between my scarf and my jacket collar, down the back of my neck, sending a shiver down my spine that chilled me to the bone. I decided right then and there that as soon as I got back to my shitty little basement apartment I was going to call my best friend Rudy, who was already living in L.A.

"When are you coming out, Mike?" was Rudy's usual question.

"As soon as I can," was my typical reply.

Except this time I called the airline as soon as I hung up the phone. That was twenty-six years ago.

I hadn't seen Rudy in almost two years but the day he took me sailing out on the Santa Monica Bay in the middle of January was the deciding factor. It was seventeen degrees, gray and miserable in New York when I left, and here we were, out on the Pacific with clear blue skies, soaking up the sun in T-shirts and shorts, kicking back, sipping Coronas. I cashed in my return ticket home and never looked back.

It wasn't like I was giving up some big, great career or anything. Hell, at the time I was driving a cab. I hadn't been doing it long, but long enough to know I didn't want to do it any longer. I'd bounced around a number of odd jobs since dropping out of Lehman College in my freshman year. Restaurant supply delivery, security guard, painter, tow truck dispatcher, I didn't take anything too seriously.

I wanted to keep my summers free so I could continue to spend them up in Maine as a sailing bum. I had been crewing on luxury sailing yachts and racing sailboats of the east coast elite since junior high. I kind of lucked into it through Rudy, whose whole family had a sort of a seafaring lifestyle and history. His dad was a boat builder—a shipwright—from Maine who moved down to City Island in the fifties to work in the Minneford Yacht Yard. Rudy's dad always sent him, his sister, and his mom up to Maine for the summer to stay with relatives, and I got lucky enough to be invited along one summer when I was thirteen years old. It didn't take anything to get my parents' permission. They must have seen it as a way to get me out of their hair for the summer. I could have told them I was going to Timbuktu and, as long as it didn't cost them anything, they were fine with it.

Rudy's uncle had a classic old Hinckley, and that first summer in Camden, they taught me the ropes. I was sort of a confused, wayward street kid at that time in my life and sailing gave me something I never got from anybody or anything else: confidence. Sailing, crewing, and maintaining sailboats was work, but it was fun work. And I worked my butt off. I was invited back the following summers, and together with Rudy, we became the "Merry Midshipmen from Morris Park." We started hiring ourselves out, first as boat cleaners—swabbies—then as sailing crew.

I was more than happy to take advantage of this life on the water. Yacht owners, particularly rich yacht owners who could afford to pay crew, weren't around all the time. So as Rudy and I got older and more experienced, we got to cruise the Penobscot Bay on some of the finest Down East sailing yachts, sometimes with their lonely wives or their hot Ivy League daughters, plus all the beer we could drink. And it was all on the captain's dime, even the beer. For a young city punk from The Bronx like myself, it was the life. I was getting paid to do something I would have gladly done for free. Rudy and I used joke around and sing the lyrics of the Dire Straits song, "Money for nothing, and the chicks for free."

After we graduated high school, we would stay on later into the Fall. We'd end the season by delivering some magnificent yacht down to the Bahamas or the Virgin Islands so their owners could spend a couple of winter weekends on them. One year we even got to stay and crew on a classic sixty-five foot Herreshoff schooner for the entire winter season in the Caribbean, then sailed it back up to Rockport the following spring. I was living the dream, getting paid and getting laid in the Caribbean in the middle of the winter while everyone else I knew was freezing their nuts off back in New York.

Rudy helped me get into the sailing life after I moved to L.A. It seems like wherever there are people with money and a body of water nearby, there are people with boats. And in L.A., there are plenty of people with money. It's always struck me as funny that people with money will always buy the most expensive boat they can get without the slightest idea of how to use it. And they sure as hell don't want to be bothered taking care of it. But they're willing to pay, and, luckily, I know how to do both. I have found that rich people are generally pretty cheap— which is probably how they got rich—but not when it comes to their boat. I've seen people who would argue over a questionable charge at a restaurant then stiff the waiter out of a tip because of it, even if they had enough money to buy the whole damn restaurant. But when you tell them they need some four-hundred-dollar fitting or some eight-hundred-dollar rigging work done on their boat, they don't even blink an eye. The checkbook comes right out.

"You ever think of getting your own boat?" I once asked Rudy as we were delivering a fifty-three foot Hallberg-Rassy up from the BVIs.

"What for? I'd only be disappointed. I'm already sailing the best boats I'd never be able to afford," was his wise response as he poured himself another margarita from the blender down below.

I, on the other hand, always dreamed of having my own boat. Because no matter how much you sail on somebody else's boat, it's always going to be somebody else's boat. And the more I sailed on somebody else's boat, the more I wanted to make it my own. Now, I didn't need some big-ass expensive yacht, with way too many electronic gadgets, bells, and whistles to break down and take care of, like my rich armchair "captains." A nice seaworthy second-hander would suit my needs perfectly—

small enough to single-hand, yet big enough to cross an ocean. A K.I.S.S. boat: Keep It Simple Stupid. I had my ideas of what I wanted for my ideal boat—a full keel, shorter single-spreader mast, cutter rig, and lighter displacement. I lucked into *Stella*, my 1989 Cabo Rico 34. I had worked and cared for her on and off for a number of years, and I knew her inside and out. I got her from the original owner, Gus, who sailed her all over the South Pacific with his wife and filled my head with dreams of doing the same. Gus owed me for a bunch of work I had done, so when his wife passed away and he realized he was getting too old to sail her alone anymore, he let me have her for a song.

I bought her about ten years ago, right after my divorce. The timing was perfect. I needed the sea again after that marriage. Pussy-whipped and virtually landlocked for eight years, I bought *Stella* and sunk some money (hidden from my ex) into fitting her out the way I wanted. I tossed my dock lines and sailed her alone, singlehandedly, around the Pacific. It was what I needed to get over the heartbreak of finding the woman who I thought was the love of my life, Sandy, banging the man who I thought was my best friend, Rudy, behind my back. It was the only time he'd ever done me wrong. But that did it.

I puttered around for months, down the coast of Mexico to Cabo San Lucas, drowning myself in tequila and cheap hookers along the way. When I got bored, I set off to the Marquesas and went island hopping all over French Polynesia. At the time, I didn't think I'd ever come back, and I wasn't really planning to. Sold everything I owned and put it in the sailing coffers. Half of me just wanted to sail off the edge of the earth. The other half answered an email I got when I found an internet connection in Papeete.

I didn't have the kind of *fuck-you* money I needed to sustain myself forever, and the coffers were already starting to run low. I suppose I could have done it down and dirty, picking up some boat work here and there. But Doug Strong had a well-paying, choice gig for me back in L.A. if I wanted it. Doug was a teamster boss, a transportation captain in the movie biz. I met him early on in my years in L.A.—Rudy and I worked on his boat. It was my foot in the door to the Hollywood Teamsters, Local 399. He had a forty-two foot Catalina, and together Rudy and I refitted and customized his cabin and navigation station according to his wild ideas. We rewired all the electronics along with his new radar, GPS, chart plotter, depth sounder, and state-of-the-art stereo. When he popped a shroud in a twenty-five knot gust on the way back from Catalina, I re-rigged his standing rigging. In return, he got me a union card and a gig driving the rescue boat for the *Beach Patrol* television series. Rudy was already in and driving the camera boat. It was like old times. It was good, easy money, and there were plenty of good-looking, bikini-clad AMW (Actress/Model/Whatever) extras who wanted to go for a boat ride.

"Welcome to below the line," Rudy quipped when I got my union card.

"What, the water line?" I asked.

Rudy explained that in the film business there were two kinds of people: Above the line and below the line. Above the line were all the mucky-mucks: the suits, the producers, the directors, the writers, the stars, and the big-money big shots. Below the line were the craftspeople, the laborers, the extras, and pretty much everyone else in show business. I told him I was happy being "below the belt."

"Not below the belt. Below the *line*," he would laughingly correct me.

"Whatever. Belt, line, if this is what it is, I'm okay with it," I replied.

I worked on the show for its last three seasons. After *Beach Patrol* wrapped, Rudy went to work driving a grip truck on a feature shooting out in San Diego. I got another below the belt gig driving a prop truck for *Hollywood Beat*, the popular TV cop show shooting here in town. That's how I first met my wife, Sandy, a set dresser, but that's another story. Eventually I learned to drive bigger rigs, even semis, making myself more marketable in the teamster circles. I started working on features and commercials too—TV shows were longer gigs but features had panache. Commercials were the shortest, but they paid the best. They were great for in between the longer gigs. Since I also knew boats—and many teamsters had boats that usually needed work—I was a popular guy. I did a lot of favors working on their boats, and in thanks, kept getting well-paid Hollywood Teamster union work.

The gig Dougie had for me was a "dream job" as he called it. It was driving Gabriella Vassey, the hot, young "A" list ingénue, to and from set for her next major motion picture. It was a cushy job and had status. Producers want to protect their investment. So when there's forty to fifty million dollars riding on a starlet's name, they not only want to take care of her, they want her protected. It was the kind of job everyone Doug knew was hitting him up for, except me. Which was one of the reasons why he wanted me. It was not the kind of gig you gave to some donut snacking, burrito packing, overweight dumb-shit, or the outlaw surfer "dude" that a lot of Hollywood movie teamster were famous for. This was a gig for someone you could trust to be professional, well mannered, and courteous, yet pack a presence of intimidation against any stalker-types or paparazzi. Plus, I cleaned up pretty well. It was more like being a glorified limousine driver-slash-bodyguard than a teamster, and you didn't have to get your hands dirty. As a matter of fact, getting your hands dirty on this gig was actually frowned upon.

Doug also told me he could also help me get a conceal-and-carry permit for the gig, something I had been wanting to get for some time. Not because I get my jollies carrying a gun, but because I can demand a higher rate. You see, lots of teamsters own their own equipment and like having someone driving for them who's going to protect their investment. Equipment like fuel trucks, stake-beds, generators, and fifth wheels are coveted by the Mexican drug cartels, and hijackings were not unusual.

Packing a piece also made me feel safer driving to remote locations, even before I had my concealed carry permit. It was also great for gigs like these, and a way to get more of them. I'd been doing USPSA shooting for some time, even won a couple of trophies and moved up in class, so I was quite proficient with a handgun. So much so that Sandy tossed my Glock 17 off the Venice pier the moment she knew I had found out about her and Rudy.

I'd be lying if I said I never toyed with the idea of taking out Sandy and Rudy. I imagine anyone who goes through a divorce with a cheating wife has the same thoughts. Living out those fantasies is what separates the crazies from the sane. Getting back at Sandy and Rudy that way wasn't worth spending the rest of my life in the can for. I couldn't blame Rudy too much. I'm sure it was Sandy who seduced him. I should have known. To think of all the times I knew they were alone together, crossing paths on work related errands or favors at our place or his. It all made sense. I was pissed it was Rudy and felt betrayed by him, but in a funny way I guess I felt like I owed Rudy for all he'd done for me over the years. Maybe I even owed him for showing me Sandy's true colors. Hell, maybe he was still trying to get back at me for banging that Boston University cheerleader Sally Walton behind his back while he was puking up Southern Comfort off the stern of the gaff-rigged schooner we were crewing on that Labor Day weekend in Bar Harbor so long ago. Maybe I'll run into him one of these days and ask him.

So I pulled *Stella*'s mast and packed her into a container to ship home before flying back to L.A. to take the ingénue gig. Through Doug's "friend" we got all my papers in order, and I received my concealed carry the day before first day of principal photography. The job itself was a piece of cake. The hardest part was getting up at three in the morning so I could haul myself up to Calabasas to pick up my starlet and get her to the make-up trailer by five.

Gabriella Vassey was fun lady, and yes, she was a lady. In

this day and age, that's hard to find. She came from Hollywood royalty. Her great-grandmother was a silent film star who made the transition to talkies by being one helluva singer and dancer in those big lavish musicals they did in the thirties. Her grandfather started out as an editor and became a staff director at Paramount during the studio days. Her father was a big time character actor and Emmy winner but drank himself to death when Gabby was still a baby. Gabby was only twenty-five when I started driving her, but she had already led more of a life than most people twice her age. She was acting when she was four and got an Oscar nomination when she was thirteen, playing a teenage runaway turned street hooker. By the time Gabby was eighteen, she had already been in and out of rehab twice and her career washed up. But she persevered. She straightened herself out and reinvented herself doing smaller indie pics. Now she was riding a wave of two blockbuster hits in a row. She commanded seven figures a picture plus a piece of the box office, and got an in-house production company deal from the studio. Yet unlike so many others in Hollywood, perhaps because of her "long," checkered life, she was genuinely down to earth and actually in touch with reality. She would rather go hiking in the Santa Monica Mountains and cook her own dinner on her weekends off than fend off the paparazzi at the latest Sunset Boulevard nightclub du jour. During our commutes, she enjoyed hearing my seafaring tales, and when the film finished shooting she gave me a Rolex Platinum Yacht Master watch as a wrap gift. The lady had class.

I thought of her as I checked the Rolex once again, still waiting for that test sail to show up. He was now over an hour late and neither he nor Corey had returned any of my calls. I had already finished walking the docks checking on my "other" boats. Boats that I was left in charge of for nominal fees or favors. Amongst other things, I was maintaining and making sure cleaning crews and bottom cleaners were doing their jobs. I had two fishing boats owned by fellow teamsters who were out of town on location for a few months, Doug Strong's new Beneteau, and a forty-nine foot Grand Banks trawler that belonged to the infamous Israeli producer, Ari Goldman. He had made his fortune in the straight-to-video European film market of the eighties and nineties. He'd been out of the country for almost a year and half now, avoiding tax collectors and the residuals department of the Screen Actors Guild. But every once in a while I would get a fat check from him to make sure his boat was well taken care of.

I decided the buyer for my boat wasn't really looking to buy, or if he was, Corey showed him something else he fell in love with. So I locked up *Stella* and walked back to my apartment across from the dock in the Tiki Marina apartment building to grab a bite and change. I was between gigs, but working tonight. Pays Lee was coming in on his private charter jet from Vegas. I had a couple of clients over the years who hired me as a freelance limo driver and bodyguard on a per diem basis.

Pays Lee was one of my regulars. He's a big time gangsta-rap record producer with his own label. Pays Lee got his name from wearing these outlandish paisley outfits. Everything he wore was paisley. He even had a line of overpriced clothing popular amongst his gangsta-rap peers. Pays started out young, in the eighties as a highly sought-after session musician. As a bass player Pays Lee played with some of the biggest and best contemporary artists before becoming a successful record producer.

Pays owed me over five thousand dollars and promised to pay up tonight. He always paid in cash, my preferred method of payment for these types of gigs. Since I still hadn't sold the boat and work had been slow, I was probably going to need it for another month of slip fees and bottom cleaning. Not to mention rent, food, and bills. Figured I'd kick back and watch the rest of the Yankee game, maybe catch a couple of Zs before heading over to Santa Monica Airport for the pick-up.

CHAPTER 2

Pays Lee likes my bulletproof Suburban. It was another perk from the Gabriella Vassey gig and another benefit of being a movie teamster. Doug Strong had it custom-made then rented it out to the production company, who was more than willing to pay the handsome rental fee to protect their investment. He made most of his money back by the time principle photography wrapped. When it did, he sold the Suburban to me for half of what it was worth. Such is the teamster life in Hollywood. It's not about the hourly rate, it's about the "kit rental" or equipment you can get on a show. Before I set out to Tahiti, I had a dually stake bed truck that paid for itself three times over on various shows in a two-year period, and I *still* got twenty-grand for it when I sold it. One of the few things my ex did not get.

Pays Lee also likes the fact I'm licensed to pack a compact 1911 .45 pistol. You see, most of these gangsta-rap types are not as tough as they seem. It's mostly an image thing, a front, and it's the real gangstas, the real bad-asses from the hood, who take advantage of them. They'll befriend the likes of Pays Lee and his "artists" and lend them some street cred by showing up at their parties and concerts, but then think nothing of ripping them off at gunpoint. The rappers and their crew would rather pay them then let word get out how chicken-shit they really were, so none of it ever gets reported. That's why they surround themselves with bodyguards and entourages, so they can hold on to some of their bread and their bling.

Pays also gets off on having a straight-looking, white guy driving him around. All his peeps had their entourage of baggy-panted, bling-bling, big-house bodybuilders backing them up. But Pays, he got himself a clean-cut, straight-looking cracker pimping his ride. And he laughs like hell when I play it up by telling him I'm "Driving Mas Pays Lee." Coming from The Bronx, I can play the street thing and rib him. Since he was originally from Queens, he eats it up. We get along and have some laughs, but I refuse to take him up on his offer for a full-time gig. The idea of hanging with him and his crew full-time does not appeal to me one iota. Real gangstas or not, he hangs with some rough dudes, no doubt about it. Prison tats and drive-bys are a way of life with them. Just because I carry a piece doesn't mean I want to have to use it. Working for Pays full time, I no doubt would have to. He already had one bodyguard take a bullet for him. No way I was taking a bullet for anyone. For the cash money he pays, I'll do some pick-ups and runs for him, but I don't want to spend too much time in his circles.

I was starting to wonder if it was because I didn't take his job offer that he was putting off paying me. Normally he'd slip me my cash as soon as I dropped him off at his Baldwin Hills crib. The fact that he was already five grand behind was starting to piss me off. I trusted him, but trust doesn't pay the bills. So as I was driving to meet his plane, I wondered how I should handle it. It had never been a problem with Pays before, but now it was becoming one.

I pulled out onto the tarmac at Santa Monica Airport as Pays' chartered G4 jet taxied its way to its hangar. I got out and stood ready as the plane's door opened and the stairway lowered to the ground. Pays' tall, slim frame filled the door in one of his signature brown paisley suits. His designer dreadlocks were pulled back into a pony-tail below his matching brown paisley driving cap. He flashed me a peace sign "V" with his fingers and he started down to stairs. Behind him a shapely, buxom, attractive young woman with long, straightened hair followed him out. My guess was she couldn't have been more than twenty or twenty-one, but I always had a hard time gauging age, particularly with African-American women. She was barely dressed in a halter top and tiniest of miniskirts, which she kept tugging down to cover herself to no avail.

As I opened the Suburban's rear passenger door, Pays smiled brightly and exchanged a fist slap with a "S'up?"

"Mister Lee." I smiled back but nodded toward the girl as she negotiated the narrow steps with her dangerously high heels.

Pays turned to her, "Let's go, girl."

"I'm coming," she giggled.

Pays smiled at me confidentially. "They call her Coffee, 'cause she grinds so fine."

I wasn't happy about this turn of events. With the girl in the car it would be hard to discuss business with Pays. He could potentially get really pissed for "dissin' him in front of one of his bitches," as he would put it. I had to hope he would play the big shot by flashing his cash around and paying me.

As the girl made it to the bottom of the stairway, it became apparent she was high as a kite as she staggered, giggling, toward the car. Pays shuffled her in before following. I swung the door closed and went to the driver's side. I got in and started driving away, and the girl was all over Pays. He let her nuzzle a bit then shoved her away when he saw me checking them out in the rear-view.

"What's the word, Mikey-Boy?"

"Same old shit. How was Vegas?"

"Good times. Always," he replied as the girl was on him again.

"How the tables treating you?" I asked, testing the money waters.

"Cold as ice," he sneered. "Damn dice gonna ruin me. Shit..."

This was not sounding good. As I tried to figure out my next move, he broached the subject. "I know I owes you, Mikey-Boy, but you're gonna have to let me slide until next time."

I shook my head and said, "That's too bad. I don't know if I can wait until next time."

The girl was all over him by this point. I couldn't see where her hand was in the rear-view, but it was pretty obvious. His eyes met mine, and he smiled at me. "You want a piece of this? She suck a mean dick."

The girl smiled in a drug-induced haze.

I shook my head and looked back at the road. "No, that's okay."

"What's a matter? You don't like the dark meat?" he persisted.

"I like it all, but that don't pay the bills."

"Shit. We call it a bonus. For having to wait. Don't affect my bill none."

"That's okay, thanks."

I kept quiet the rest of the way to Pays' crib while he got serviced and satisfied in the back seat. When I dropped him off, he shut the door before the girl could get out.

"Whoa, what gives?" I said.

"Yo, take the bitch to my boy Butch's crib and put it on my tab," he said.

"You know, Pays, it would be one thing if you were paying me but..."

"It's cool. Listen...come by my office tomorrow, and I'll have a check for you."

"This is supposed to be a C.O.D. arrangement," I reminded him.

"It's all good. Pop by my office tomorrow, and I'll square it all up."

I didn't believe him, but I didn't really have a choice. I looked back at the girl through the window. She was passed out. "Where am I taking her?"

Pays took out a pen, jotted down an address on one of his business cards, and handed it to me. "Don't worry. It's cool. I'll see you tomorrow," as he headed toward the door of his luxury

Baldwin Hills mansion. I looked down at the address. Inglewood. Checking my watch, I thought, "Great! Just where I want to be at 2:00 a.m. with a passed out black chick in my car."

As I made my way to Inglewood, I tried to play out the scenario that would take place at Pays' office if I didn't get paid. What could I do? How could I collect if push came to shove? The more I thought about it, the more pissed off I got. I finally pulled up to a home in a decent-looking neighborhood on the edge of the hood. Luckily no one was hanging out on the street or the neighboring porches. This would not have been an uncommon sight in this neck of the woods, no matter what time of night.

The girl was still passed out, so I got out of the car and approached the house. The house was dark. I checked the address and checked my piece before ringing the bell. I had to ring a couple of times before the porch light came on and someone eyed me from the front door window.

"Pays Lee sent me," I told him.

The door opened a crack and the muscle-bound, jet black Butch, dressed in nothing but boxer shorts, gave me the once over while making sure I saw the pistol in his hand.

"What you want?"

"Pays Lee told me to drop off a girl here," I told him.

"What girl?"

I suddenly realized I didn't know her name. "She's in the car. Pays said they call her Coffee, 'cause she grinds so fine."

"Uh-uh. She can't come in. I got my old lady here."

"Hey, this is where Pays told me to drop her. You can take it up with him," I turned toward the Suburban.

"Yo!"

I turned back and found myself looking down the barrel of his .40 cal. "I said get the bitch outta here! You understand?"

Gangsta rappers! *Pays Lee is going to pay for this* I thought as I put my hands up in surrender. "Yeah, okay. No problem." I backed away slowly to the Suburban.

When I got in, I dialed Pays on my cell phone and started the car. Butch had shut the door and turned out the light, but I still pulled away to get out of range. Pays didn't answer so I tried again. After the third time, I stopped myself from sending a very pissed-off text message and simply wrote, "Butch wouldn't take her. Call me."

I pulled over, reached back, and tried to rouse the girl, but she was out like a light. I was about to get out and try harder but thought better of it when I saw a police cruiser drive by. A white guy dragging a scantily-dressed black girl out of his car in this neighborhood in the middle of the night would not look good. I thought about bringing her back to Pays' pad and dumping her on his front steps if he didn't answer the door. But, again, a white guy dragging a black girl out of his car in the middle of the night in an upscale black neighborhood didn't look too good either. I decided to get the hell out of Inglewood and head back to Marina del Rey. It would be dead there at this time of night and I figured I could get her on my boat, make her some coffee, and get an address where to take her.

I got back to the marina, happy to see it was dead quiet, no sign of life. It was not uncommon to see some all-night, booze fest on some live-aboard boat. I parked the Suburban as close as I could to the dock gate and tried to shake awake the girl in the back seat. She nudged me and moaned but was still out like a light. Looking around one more time to make sure there were no prying eyes or late-night dog walkers, I reached in, grabbed her, pulled her out, and tossed her over my shoulder. I tried in vain to tug on her tiny miniskirt as it rode up leaving nothing to the imagination. It wasn't working so I hurried, unlocked the gate, and scurried down the dock to *Stella* with the girl's ass next to my face. Once aboard, I had to set her aside on the cockpit bench while I opened the companionway hatch-boards. I waited until I got her below and laid her out on the settee before I turned on a light.

This was the first really good look I got of her. Besides her buxom, shapely, young body, she actually had a very pretty face. Seeing her sleeping made her look young and innocent. She didn't seem to possess that ghetto, street harshness that was typical with the likes of Pays Lee and his crowd. I covered her with a light blanket that wasn't too moldy, set up the coffee and was about to start it when I decided to take breather. It was late. I was tired. And there was no way I was getting this girl up any time soon. I sat back on the opposite settee and closed my eyes.

I awoke to the sound of retching coming from the head. It took me a few moments to think who could be in the bathroom before I remembered the girl. When the coughing stopped, I got up to check on her.

"You all right?"

"Where am I?" She replied in a hung-over, hazy voice.

"You're on my boat, in Marina del Rey. You remember Pays Lee leaving you with me?" I asked.

"I remember being in Las Vegas...what time is it?"

I checked my watch and replied, "Seven-ten. Want me to take you home?"

"What's today?" she suddenly asked in a panic.

"Monday."

"Oh my god, I've got to get to school."

"I can drop you off..."

She looked down at her outfit, "My clothes. Where are my clothes?"

"That's what you were wearing when I picked you up. You and Pays Lee. Don't you remember?" I told her all I knew. I could see her trying to put the pieces together through her clouded brain.

"My mother's going to kill me!" She started to cry.

This was going from bad to worse with the mention of mom and the waterworks. I was not liking this, but I tried to play it cool and calm her down.

"Look, it's going to be all right. I'll take you whereever you need to go."

"I can't go like this!" she said, waving her hands in front of her outfit. She crossed her arms in front of her, covering her halter-top breasts.

I turned away and pointed toward a cabinet, "There's some spare clothes in there, help yourself."

She threw open the door and grabbed one of my denim work shirts that was roughly three sizes too big for her. She put it on wrapping it tightly around her.

"I can't go to school like this," she said.

She explained that her mother thought she was staying at a friend's then straight to school. If she didn't show up, they'd call her mother to find out where she was.

I was afraid to ask, but I did. "What school you go to?" I was hoping she'd say some junior college or one of the Cal State universities.

"Crosswinds."

"Crosswinds? As in Crosswinds Academy?" *Yikes*, I thought. Crosswinds is a high school. "How old are you?"

"Fifteen."

Fifteen! This called for some fast thinking. I turned on the coffee and told her to wait there below while I went up on deck and made a couple of calls.

Crosswinds Academy was an upscale private school in Brentwood. Her parents were either very well-to-do or she was one of their affirmative action, attempt-at-diversity students. Either way, I wanted to wash my hands of her as fast as I could.

Cursing Pays Lee when he wouldn't pick up, I tried my buddy, Jimmy Sheehan. He was an assistant director, but his wife was a wardrobe mistress. If his wife, Molly, was working, she might have some clothes I could borrow that would be suitable for a fifteen-year-old.

"This is Jimmy," he answered after one ring.

"Jimbo, it's Mike Millek. You working?"

Turns out Jimmy was on set of the new George Rossi movie at the Sony lot. He couldn't talk, so I asked him quickly if his wife was on the show.

"Yeah, why?" He sounded suspicious or jealous or both.

"I need a favor. Can you give me her number?" I asked, trying to be as brief as possible. I told him I was in a jam and needed an outfit for chick I picked up, which was sort of the truth.

"What's the matter, she doesn't want to do the walk of shame?" he laughed.

"You got it." I went along with it and told him I'd catch up later.

He gave me her number then said, "Hey, listen. Just so you know, Molly and me, we uh, we split up. We're getting a divorce."

"Shit, I'm sorry, Jimmy. I had no idea."

"Yeah, well, shit happens, I guess."

"Yeah, I can relate."

After an awkward pause, he said, "Anyway, I wanted you to hear from me. I gotta run."

"You okay with me calling her?" I asked.

"Yeah, yeah, don't worry about it."

"Okay, thanks. I'll catch you later." I hung up.

I reflected on what Jimmy had told me as I dialed his soon to be ex-wife. Not exactly unexpected in this business. Most of the people my age I knew in the business were either divorced, getting divorced, or on their second or third marriage. Came with the territory, I guess. Somebody cheated on somebody and pride wouldn't let them work it out. It's a funny thing working in the biz. You work long, hard hours with a bunch of people, with a lot of waiting around getting to know each other. Usually for a month or three at a time, sometimes out of town, on location, and you get...close. Like family close. Like relationship close. Things happen. Sparks fly. It happened with Sandy and me. It happened with Sandy and Rudy. I wondered who cheated, Jimmy or Molly. Jimmy was no angel. I remembered working on a show with him years ago, before he was married, and he was banging a make-up girl and a camera assistant on the same show.

Jimmy's wife, Molly, was a dish. I've known her for years, and I swear she got better looking the older she got. Like a fine wine, she got better with age. Her hair was somewhere between a blond and a redhead. Strawberry blond, I've heard it called. A green-eyed, strawberry blonde with freckles that ran down from her face to her chest and disappeared into her ample, but not overbearing cleavage. I'd be lying if I said I never had the hots for her. Hell, I always had the hots for her. I'd like to think there was some unspoken heat between us, but because she was married to Jimmy, I never pursued it. I weighed the possibilities now that they were splitting up. I thought about those freckles as I dialed her number.

"Molly, Mike Millek, how're you doing?"

"Hey handsome, long time, no see. Where you been hiding?" she asked.

"I'll tell you when I see you," and explained my situation. Or at least the one I'd let Jimmy assume.

As luck would have it, they were shooting a big scene that day with about seventy-five extras. Molly and her crew had to dress them all, so she had tons of different outfits in all different sizes. She told me to come by and she'd hook me up.

I hung up, went below, and poured some coffee in a to-go mug then poured some for the girl. I asked her what her size was and told her I'd be back within the hour. The Sony lot was only about fifteen minutes away from Marina del Rey at this hour. I headed out, but as an afterthought, I turned and asked the girl her name.

"Lauren," she said.

"Okay, Lauren. I'm Mike. Listen, don't worry about a thing. Just stay here, out of sight, and we'll get this all worked out."

She rubbed her temple and simply said, "Thank you."

CHAPTER 3

The Sony lot was all abuzz. It was only the second week of shooting and the George Rossi film was taking up three sound stages. It was another one of his big-budget super-hero movies so there were enormous sets plus one stage devoted entirely to green screen work. Molly had arranged for my drive-on pass, and I was able to pull my Suburban right up next to the wardrobe trailer. As I got out, I heard a familiar voice call my name—Chris DeLuca, the transpo' captain on the show. Chris was the walking definition of barrel-chested. Short, stocky, dark curly hair and beard, he was a bull.

"What's up, Chris?" I asked. He walked up and we shook hands.

"I was just about to call you," he lied.

"Really?"

"I'm looking for another day player for today. You available?"

Shit, I thought. An opportunity for a day's pay, and I'm still playing cleanup to that deadbeat Pays Lee's mess. I tried to see if I could salvage the situation.

"I'm in the middle of a something right now, but I'll be available in about an hour," I said.

"I need somebody to pick up a honey wagon in Burbank, ASAP," he said checking his watch.

"I can have it here before noon," I said still trying.

"That's okay. Good to see you." He started to walk away,

tapping a number on his cell phone.

"I'm around if you need me. Just day-playing these days," I said, trying not to sound too desperate.

"I'll call you," he said while I watched him walk off.

At that moment I got goosed with a slap on my rear end.

"Hey, sweetcakes, where you been?"

I turned to see a smiling Molly with an arm full of dresses and a tape measure around her neck. She was frazzled but looked great. Her button-down shirt was open just enough to see those freckles disappearing beneath it.

"Too far away, obviously."

I threw an arm around her and gave her a peck on the cheek.

"Let me help you," I said and took the dresses from her, following her into the trailer.

"Thanks. So, I guess you heard about Jimmy and me?"

"Yeah. That was a surprise. I'm sorry to hear that."

She took the dresses one by one and hung them up. Her trailer was basically a forty-foot closet with a fitting room, washer and dryer, ironing board, and clothes steamer.

"Don't be. I'm not." She turned and looked me in the eye. "The fucker denies me a child for eleven years then knocks up some twenty-three-year-old P.A. and suddenly he wants to be a father. What the hell is that all about?"

At a loss for words, I shook my head and shrugged. "I'm sorry, Molly," I repeated.

She gave me an "all men are scum" look before asking, "So, who's this girl you're fooling around with?"

"It's not like that. She got dumped on me on a job. I'm just trying to get her outta my hair."

"That's not how Jimmy put it."

"I had to tell him something to get your number," I winked.

She smiled at that. "So what do you need?"

"Oh, you know, something daytime casual. What a…young lady might wear to an upscale private school."

Molly gave me a dirty look. "You too?"

24

"I told you it's not like that."

"Any idea what size?"

I gave her Laurel's sizes and she put together a couple of young, collegiate-looking ensembles. She told me to bring back whatever I didn't use.

"You know this is going to cost you."

"No problem." I asked as I reached into my pants.

"What are you doing?

"What? How much I owe you?"

"I don't want your money," she said as if I insulted her.

"Then what?"

"I want you to take me sailing."

"What?"

"You heard me."

"Seriously?" I smiled.

"Yeah. That's all you ever talked about. Sailing. And you never invited me out on your boat. So, take me out on the water, sailor boy."

I was hesitant to commit because I didn't want to cause any friction with Jimmy, a potential employer. But those freckles were staring me in the face.

"Okay, sure," I said, thinking it would probably never happen anyway.

A production assistant with a walkie-talkie then knocked and came in with three extras.

"Three more for the restaurant scene," she informed Molly.

Molly sized up the extras and started searching the racks of clothes, and I took it as my cue to leave. I held up the outfits she gave me and said, "Thanks Mol, I'll catch you later."

"Don't forget. I'm going to hold you to it."

"Don't worry."

I made it half the twelve steps back to my Suburban before I ran into the suave, svelte Jimmy dressed impeccably in high-end casual wear, complete with one of his signature vintage, retro neckties. It was a bit of pretention on his part but also a tribute to old Hollywood when that was the thing. As usual he was wearing his walkie-talkie headset and barking orders. He smiled and held up a finger at me to wait while he finished his transmission.

"Copy that, tell him we need it ASAP on Stage Two for the next set-up." With that, he extended his hand to me. "How's it going, Mikey? I see Molly took care of you."

"Yeah. Good. I hear you're going to be a father?"

"You believe that?"

"Congratulations."

"Thanks, man. It's all good."

I wasn't sure where to take the conversation and was saved when he received another transmission in his earpiece.

"The jib's on its way over from Stage Three. Is Julie done with make-up yet, over?" he replied.

I held out my hand, and we shook again.

"Let's grab a beer when you have time, and catch up," I offered.

"Copy that" he said into his walkie before saying to me, "Sounds good. I'll call you." Then he was off, tending to one of the million things a first assistant director has to contend with.

I checked my watch, and I jumped in the Suburban before I ran into anyone else I might know.

I flew down Washington Boulevard and made it back to the marina in ten minutes flat. I parked right at the head of the dock, bolted down the gangway, and hopped aboard *Stella*. As soon as I got below, I saw that Lauren was gone. My immediate reaction was panic that she fell overboard. I ran back up on deck and scanned the waters around the dock. No sign of her. I backtracked up the dock to the parking lot, scouring the area as I went. I checked the dockside restroom and showers to see if she was cleaning herself up, but again, no sign of her. I walked around the entire Tiki Marina apartment building complex, eying every doorway, garage entrance, nook, and cranny, but could not find her. I had been gone just under an hour, so she could be anywhere. I could not believe she had vanished when I told her to stay put.

It was almost nine when I spotted the apartment manager, Liz Blanco, arriving for work. Liz was a raven-haired beauty, an amateur triathlete. She had the hard body and shapely legs under her business suit and skirt to show for it. We got along pretty well since her husband was a low-budget film producer, and I had helped him out a couple of times, getting him a deal on some equipment he needed.

Like most of the buildings in the marina, the Tiki Marina Apartments and Docks had recently completed a major renovation, updating its look from the original swinging-sixties, pseudo-Polynesian, stucco façade. One of the improvements was a new security system with numerous cameras around the building and on the docks. I thought maybe I could sweet-talk Liz into letting me view the video footage from the last hour. Liz is good people, and I'd done some work on her and her husband's boat, an old Columbia thirty-footer. I was a little nervous of what the video might show, so I had to approach this carefully. She took great pride in keeping the building's reputation clean, cozy, and scandal-free. Being another woman of my fantasies, as well as my landlord, I had to be diplomatic as well as pragmatic. I trotted up beside her as she approached the front door.

"'Morning, Liz, let me help you," I said, as I grabbed a shopping bag she was carrying.

"Hey, Mike, thanks." She smiled.

We traded small talk as I walked her to her office right off the lobby. Her bubbly assistant, Geraldine, was already at her desk and on the phone. She smiled brightly and waved enthusiastically as I walked by. Once inside her office, she turned to me and asked straight out, "What's up, Mike?"

"I need a favor," I told her.

"The wet-vac again? I'll have Javier bring it out to you."

I had borrowed the building's wet vacuum a couple of times when my automatic bilge pump went on the fritz.

"No, it's not that," I said. I asked her if it was possible to watch the security video from the previous hour or so around my dock. I made up story about misplacing my power drill somewhere between my boat, my car, and the building entrance near my apartment and that it was driving me crazy. Maybe watching the video would help me find it?

She looked anxious to get to work so she set me up on the computer in the dock master's office. She gave me a quick tutorial on the various camera angles and how to rewind and zoom in. As she was rewinding the camera angle of my dock, Geraldine stuck her head in to tell her that her 9:30 a.m. lease signing was there. Liz checked her watch.

"He's early. Tell him I'll be with him in a couple of minutes." As Geraldine left, Liz shook her head and said to me, "Why can't people just show up on time? I haven't even had my coffee yet."

I saw this as a break, "Why don't you go? I think I got this."

"You sure?"

"Yeah, go ahead."

"Want some coffee?"

"I'm okay," I told her, even though I was dying for some. But I wanted to get her out of the room so she wouldn't see the scantily clad, under-age Lauren leaving my boat.

I found the angle showing my dock and backed up the video until I saw myself leaving for the Sony lot. The day's date and the time—7:34 a.m.—showed in the bottom corner of the screen. I played the video forward at double speed until I saw Lauren, wearing my old oversized denim shirt tied at the waist, stumble off *Stella,* and negotiate the floating dock barefoot and carrying her high-heels, at 7:49 a.m. I waited until she walked off screen then picked her up on another camera angle walking through the parking area toward the front of the building. When she turned the corner, I picked her up on yet another camera angle.

Javier, the janitor, was working on what looked like a

sprinkler head at the edge of the garden near the entrance. I slowed down the video to normal speed and watched as she spoke to him. Javier nodded, took out his cell phone, and handed it to her. She made a call and Javier went back to his task. She had her back to the camera, but in the middle of her call, she must have asked Javier something because he looked up and spoke to her. She finished the call and handed the phone back to Javier. They chatted for a moment and Javier pointed off in the direction of the entrance to the driveway. Lauren headed that way. The clock on the screen read 7:53 a.m.

I scanned the other camera angles until I saw her exit the driveway and sit down on the curb next to one of the Tiki statues that flanked the entrance, elbows on her knees and head in her hand. I sped up the video and she stayed that way for over half an hour, barely moving except to scan the street when a car came by. At 8:37 a.m., she got to her feet. A late-model, black Mercedes-Maybach S600 pulled up and she got in. I tried to manipulate the zoom to see if I could get a license plate number, but the angle was wrong and too far away to get a sharp view. I tried some other angles near the entrance but no luck. Tiki Marina even had a camera on back of one of the statues specifically focused on the backs of cars entering so they'd capture license plates of every car entering the property. But since the Maybach never entered the property, I couldn't get a good look. I watched some more at double speed until I saw my Suburban pull in at 8:42 a.m. I must have passed the Maybach going in the opposite direction on Admiralty Way.

Liz then popped back in and asked, "Find your drill?"

"Uh, no. I didn't. I must have left it on the boat," I said. "Thanks anyway."

"No problem."

As I got up and was about to leave, I asked her, "Do you know where Javier is? I may need to see if I can borrow his."

"I'll call him." I followed her back to her office where she picked up a walkie-talkie and called Javier. She spoke to him in

Spanish then informed me he was working on the C-dock restrooms.

"You want me to have him bring it over to your boat?" she asked.

"That's okay I'll walk over there," I replied. "Thanks again," I said and headed out the door.

I found Javier loading up his golf cart with his plumbing tools at the dockside restrooms on the C dock. I questioned him about the girl in half English and my poor Spanish.

"Si, si, she use my phone," and he pulled it out of his pocket.

I asked him if I could see it and checked the number she called. It was a 310 area code, so I knew it was on the west side. I didn't have anything to write it down with so I took a picture of the number with my phone.

I asked him what they talked about, and he said that she asked for the building address. That made sense if she were calling someone to pick her up.

"Gracias, Javier," I told him. As an afterthought, I pulled a twenty out of my pocket and shoved it in his hand with the phone. He tried to give it back, but I shook my head no, put my finger to my lips in a "shh" gesture, and winked. Javier nodded.

"Si, no se habla." He smiled.

"No habla Senorita Blanco," I smiled back.

"Si, si," he said as he pocketed the twenty.

I went back into the building and headed for my apartment. The long night was catching up to me. I figured I'd see if I could Google the phone number and find out who she called.

By time I got back to my apartment and plopped down on the couch, I didn't care anymore about who picked up Lauren. She was out of my hair, and figured I should just wash my hands of the whole thing. I thought I'd catch a few Zs then head over to Pays Lee's office and shake his money tree. On the way, I'd stop by the Sony lot to return Molly's loaner outfits. I kicked off my shoes, laid back on the couch, and before I knew it, I was out like a light.

CHAPTER 4

I woke up right before 2:00 p.m. to my phone ringing. The caller ID said it was Chris DeLuca, so I picked up.

"What's up, Chris?" I asked trying to sound awake.

"Hey, Mike, you available the next couple days?" he asked. "I could use an extra driver with half a brain here at the lot."

"Uh, yeah, hold on one second…let me check something," I said, trying not to sound too desperate for the work. I put the phone down and rubbed the sleep out of my eyes. "Yeah, no, nothing I can't get out of if you need me. What's the rate like?"

"This ain't no country club gig like you're used to," he ribbed me. "But I can get you four for ten. We'll probably be doing twelve to fourteen."

That translated to four hundred dollars for a ten-hour day, plus two hours overtime for a twelve-hour day at time and a half. That came to five hundred twenty dollars a day, or six hundred eighty dollars for a fourteen-hour day, with two hours of double time.

"Can I get the Suburban on?" I asked to see if I could get a "kit" rental fee on top of my salary.

"Not this time. I need you for van shuttle."

"No problem. Count me in. What time is call?"

Chris filled me in on the details of where and when to meet. I would be running a shuttle between the off-studio lot employee parking and the studio stages. A big production like this George

Rossi picture could have as many as a hundred crew people plus cast, not to mention all the extras. The Sony lot didn't have enough on-site parking for everyone so they needed to be shuttled in. After Chris gave me the particulars—and a 4:30 a.m. call time—he started in on small talk.

"You still do work for that Pays Lee rapper guy?" he asked.

"Occasionally. He offered me a full-time gig, but I can only handle him and his crew in small doses if you know what I mean."

"I hear you. The reason I asked is that I heard your old buddy Rudy was working for him too."

I couldn't tell if Chris was needling me or merely relaying scuttlebutt. This was news to me, and I wasn't sure what it meant. Was Rudy the reason I wasn't getting paid? I couldn't figure out why that would be but who knows. I got up and decided to make some coffee so I could think and wash the cobwebs from my brain. I decided to take the high road with Chris and said, "Well, good for him. Pays pays well, when he pays."

Chris laughed as I checked my watch thinking I still wanted to get to Pays' office to see if I could actually get a check out of him.

"When was the last time you saw Rudy?" Chris asked.

"Years. Yeah, I'm surprised we haven't crossed paths."

"I heard he and Sandy split up."

"Really? Well, I guess that doesn't surprise me too much."

"You still hold a grudge?" he asked.

"As far as I can tell, he did me a favor," I said, high-roading it again.

I didn't know where Chris was heading with this conversation, digging up old dirt from my past. But he got to his point. "So would you be okay working together again? 'Cause he might be sharing some days with you."

It threw me but I didn't want to blow the work. I replied quickly, "I've got no problem with that as long as he doesn't. And I don't know why he should."

"Okay. Well, I didn't want to surprise you or have any shit stirred up on the lot."

I told Chris that I appreciated the heads-up but that he didn't have to worry about me stirring up anything. We caught up for a couple minutes more about other old friends who were on the show then ending with goodbyes and seeya tomorrows.

I poured myself a cup of coffee, still thinking about the conversation and the mention of Rudy, and headed for the shower.

I dressed in my black, limo-driver suit. Pays didn't much care how I dressed for his late-night pick-ups but during the day, or during clubbing hours, he wanted me to play the limo driver. Since I was showing up at his office in the middle of the afternoon I didn't want to give him any excuse to put off paying me.

By 3:00 p.m. I was in the Suburban heading into Pays Lee's Hollywood office. Not a good time of day to be heading east. I knew the traffic both going there and coming back was going to suck. I thought maybe I'd grab a bite or catch a movie on that side of town to wait out the rush hour traffic on the way home. I needed to make it an early night seeing I had to get my ass out of bed and be at the Sony lot by the rude hour of 4:30 a.m. I decided to wait until tomorrow to return Molly's loaners since I was going to be on the lot anyway. The thought of seeing her the next couple of days gave me something to look forward to. I wasn't so sure how I felt about seeing Rudy.

As I made my way up the 405 freeway toward the 10, I heard something strange coming from the back seat. It sounded like some musical scratch riff that gets repeated over and over in rap songs. Since traffic was crawling, I reached around and dug something out from under the passenger seat. It was a small woman's purse. It had to be Lauren's. I had no idea she even had a bag with her. I had actually forgotten all about her until that moment. I dug around inside the purse and found the source of the sound—the ringtone on her iPhone. The caller ID read, "MOM." Before I could think what to do, the ringing stopped, and I assumed it went to voice mail. I went through the bag as I crawled on the exit ramp to the 10 East. Not much—a bottle of perfume, some mints, an e-cigarette, a pack of condoms, and a small billfold. I went through the billfold and found Lauren's Crosswinds student ID, a debit card, and a couple of business cards, one for Pays Lees Productions and one for the law firm of Pichter, Loam, and Stein. Everyone in town knew Pichter, Loam, and Stein as Hollywood power brokers and lawyers for a number of elite A-list stars. As I tried to figure out what Lauren might be doing with a Pichter, Loam, and Stein business card in her purse, the phone rang again. As before, it read "MOM." I hit the accept button and listened.

"Lauren, is that you?" The attitude and southern accent made it sound like the voice of an angry middle-aged black woman. "Answer me! Where are you? I know you didn't go to school today!"

I continued to listen to see if I could get any information from the call. It did not seem good that Lauren never made it to school. Her mom was obviously worried about her safety. It made me begin to worry myself.

"Lauren, are you there or not?"

Her mother must have assumed the call was lost and she hung up. The phone rang again, but I didn't answer. After it went to voicemail, I tried to access her call log but her phone was locked. Checking her school ID again, I tried the last four digits of her student ID number figuring it was probably her social security number. No luck. Date of birth? There it was: May 6, 2005. I tried 5605 and I was in.

I pulled off the La Cienega exit and got caught at a light. I sat there and went through the call log to see "MOM" had called about ten times today, including the last couple of calls. Not good. I decided to see who Lauren had called but the light turned green. I drove up La Cienega trying to figure out my next move. I wanted to make sure she was okay so nothing could come back to haunt me, but I also wanted to keep my distance. Wait a second...I pulled over and jammed on the brakes. Her student ID. Lauren Bartley! Was she the love child of Michelle Bartley? The same Michelle Bartley who was the top ten Grammy winning diva cum actress cum crack addict cum rehabbed, reformed gospel singer cum wife of power broker lawyer Jonathan Pichter? That would certainly explain the Pichter, Loam, and Stein business card.

Michelle Bartley was on top of the charts for most of the nineties and early aughts with her soulful, silken voice and incredible good looks. Gabriella Vassey used to listen to her all the time. Hollywood grabbed hold of her and starred her in a couple of cheesy love stories playing singers so they could throw in some reason for her to sing a couple of songs. It was around this time she gave birth to the love child I was now thinking was Lauren. She received critical acclaim for playing blues legend Bessie Wallace in the biopic but failed to garner an Oscar nomination. A lot of Hollywood insiders thought she could have and should have won. There were rumors that someone inside the academy kept the nomination from her. Some say it was racially motivated, but who knows. Whatever the reason, it was what sent her spiraling down the crack cocaine path. She hit rock bottom when she passed out on stage during a concert at the Hollywood Bowl. After that, nobody would touch her, the Hollywood curse so many have been dealt.

Jonathan Pichter had been Michelle's lawyer, and took pity on her. He got her into rehab and cleaned her up. He sent her back to Mississippi, to the church she grew up in to sing gospel. She supposedly found God, and it helped save her. Pichter brought her back to Hollywood, married her, and moved her and her daughter into his Brentwood Home. A powerful white Jewish lawyer marries a black former superstar, drug addict diva slash born-again gospel singer, and lives happily ever after. Only in Hollywood.

I put the Pichter, Loam, and Stein card in my pocket, turned off the phone, and stuffed it in Lauren's bag before stashing the bag back under the seat as I pulled into the garage on Sunset for Pays Lee's office.

CHAPTER 5

I went up the elevator to Pays Lee's floor and strolled into the glassed-off reception area. There were large video screens set up around the waiting area playing rap videos of Pays Lee's latest "artists." The huge window behind the reception desk displayed a panoramic view of the Sunset Strip and the Hollywood Hills. The receptionist was a slim, attractive African-American woman, probably in her thirties, I'm guessing, with an Angela Davis Afro right out of the sixties. I'd only been to Pays' office once before so I doubted she remembered me, but I tried playing it familiar even though I couldn't remember her name.

"How you doin'?" I smiled.

"Can I help you?" she replied, pleasantly though not very warmly.

"Yes. I'm sorry I forgot your name. I'm Mike. Mike Millek," I extended my hand.

"Kaneesha," she said and shook it briefly, giving me a hesitant look.

"Right, Kaneesha! I'm Mister Lee's Vegas pick-up driver. He asked me to come by to pick up a check."

"Millek, you say?" she asked as she looked through some envelopes.

"Mike. Mike Millek."

"I'm sorry, I don't have anything for you."

"That's strange. I picked up Mister Lee last night and he told

37

me to come by the office today to pick it up."

She gave me a look that said, *I've heard that before.*

"Is Mister Lee around? Perhaps I can talk to him?"

The phone rang as she pointed to the waiting area.

"Mister Lee is in a meeting right now. If you'd like to wait I'll see what I can do."

She answered the phone before I could get another word in. I mouthed "Thank you" before turning to the waiting area. There I got hit with the pungent aroma of some serious stinkweed. Seated on one of the leather sofas with serious man-spread were three brothers in designer sweat suits, baseball hats, sunglasses, and enough bling to open up a small jewelry store. All of their bloodshot eyes were on me as I settled in on the sofa across from them, beside the only other white guy in the waiting area. He had his back to me and them, talking on his cell phone. One of the brothers lit up a big spliff and passed it to his neighbor.

"S'up?" I nodded.

They ignored me and went back to smoking and watching the video screen where a couple of rappers mugged it up to a camera surrounded by shapely vixens shaking their booties. As if we hadn't seen a rap video like that before. I wondered if Pays Lee owed this crew some money or if they were "artists" here to audition.

"How much does he owe you?" a voice beside me asked.

I turned and came face to face with Rudy pocketing his cell phone. I was totally taken back, didn't know if I should be happy to see him or angry. I tried to play it cool and test the waters, "Enough to drag me over here," I replied.

"Well, take a number."

I nodded. "How much does he owe you?"

He indicated the video screens and said, "Enough to keep me sitting here listening to this shit for over an hour."

I smiled and glanced over at the crew who gave us both a dirty look. I told Rudy, "Yeah, my bill just went up."

Rudy was looking trim and fit as I remember him. His hair,

like mine was starting to gray and he sported the fashionable three-day beard. He was dressed casually in jeans, a colorful Hawaiian shirt, and flip-flops. Eying my suit he asked, "You going to a funeral?"

"Just got off a job," I lied suddenly feeling way overdressed.

"So, how you been?" Rudy asked.

"Fine." I still wasn't sure how I felt so it took a moment before I asked him back, "You?"

"All right. I hear we might be working together," he mentioned.

"So I hear."

"You okay with that?" he asked.

"You going to bow out if I'm not?"

"Fuck no."

"Then I guess it doesn't make a difference."

"I guess not," he said.

There was some awkward silence as we stared vacantly at the video screens. The rappers on them now cruised the 'hood in low-riders.

"So, how's Sandy?" I finally asked, stealing a glance out of the corner of my eye.

"I don't know, and I don't give a shit." He then turned to me and said, "We split up over a year ago. Found out she was fucking some other guy."

I smiled and said, "Welcome to the club." This broke the ice, and we both chuckled. I thought of egging him on, saying that I hoped it was with his best friend, but I decided not to. He was with Sandy longer than I was, so he must have been hurting at least as much as I was back when. I decided to let sleeping dogs lie. Besides, it felt kind of good to see him again.

I nodded toward the crew and asked, "How long the Jackson Three been waiting?"

Rudy shrugged, "Been here since I got here. That's the third joint they've smoked since. Already got a contact buzz."

I decided to do something I would have done years ago

hanging out with Rudy. I turned to the crew brother that was presently toking, smiled, and asked, "You got a prescription for that?"

He smiled back and said, "Don't need none." His crew-members snickered and laughed.

"That's right, the shit's legal now," I nodded. "Hey, can I get a hit?"

It took them by surprise that some cracker in a suit would have the balls to ask for a toke. They exchanged looks, laughed, and passed me the joint. Instead of taking a hit, I turned and butted it out in the plant next to the couch.

Before they could protest, I turned back to them and said, "Sorry, dude, I can't take the secondhand smoke. If you want to smoke, go outside."

I could tell they were all appalled as they replied with some choice expletives. I ignored them and turned back to Rudy. He was laughing.

I started laughing too. "What? Am I wrong? You can't be smoking in office buildings anymore."

The crew was then called in to whomever they were meeting with. They were still muttering, tsking, and looking over their shoulder at us as they were led to the back offices. Before the last one disappeared through the door, he turned and gave me the finger. This made me and Rudy laugh more.

We started to reminisce about old times, pre-Sandy and pre-California, back in our sailing adventure days. "Remember the Lusty Mermaid?" he asked, reminding me about a delivery we did from Rhode Island to Bermuda with the owner's hot, sex-crazed, nympho wife. We weren't a day out of Newport before she was doing both of us on our off-watches. She pulled her weight as a crewmember, but she also fucked and sucked the shit out of both of us the whole way down there. I remember when we arrived at St. George's Harbor, Rudy and I wanted to hurry the hell out of there before her husband showed up. We didn't think we'd be able to hide the fact that we were screwing his wife day and night for the previous ten days. Turned out he got there ahead of us, thanked us for taking care of his wife, and gave us each a hundred-dollar tip before dropping us off at the airport for our flight back to New York.

We talked about the good times we had together in California before Sandy. We talked about the movies and shows we'd worked on and the people we knew, catching up on who'd seen who and who was doing what.

An hour passed before we realized we'd been sitting there without hearing anything from Pays Lee or even an offer of water or coffee. I took out my cell phone and called the receptionist. I could hear the phone ring across the room.

"Pays Lee Productions."

"Hi Kaneesha, this is Mike Millek from the waiting area..." I started.

She snapped her head in our direction as I continued.

"Is it possible to get a cup of coffee and a bottle of water, please?"

The receptionist hung up and punched a number on the phone, followed by some whispering into the phone. After she hung up, she shouted across the room to us. "Mister Lee's assistant will be out in a minute to see you."

"Thanks," I called back. "I'll take the coffee black," I added as an afterthought.

Rudy was still smiling. A minute later, Omar, Pays Lee's three-hundred-pound "assistant" came out to see us. Omar wasn't much for muscle but his sheer size and stature was intimidating enough to act as muscle. I'd known Omar before while driving Pays and we'd gotten along, so I thought I could be straight with him.

"Hey, Omar, what gives?"

"Mike, whatcha doing here?"

"Pays told me to come by to collect on some money he owes me."

Omar looked over at Rudy. I could tell they knew each other

as well.

"Same here, Omar. Been waiting patiently over two hours."

"We just want to get paid," I said. "Can you talk to the man for us?"

"You got an invoice?" he asked. We both pulled out fresh invoices folded in envelopes and handed them to Omar.

He took them, sighed and said, "Lemme see what I can do," before ambling off, taking his time, disappearing into the back offices.

Five minutes later Omar returned empty-handed.

"Mister Lee says he'll have a check for you both in the mail by the end of the week," he said.

That got both Rudy and me to our feet.

"Are you kidding?" said Rudy.

"Come on, Omar," I said. You know that's bullshit. He told us to come down here."

Omar held his hands out. "That's what the man said, so, that's what the man said."

Rudy and I looked at each other, frustrated. We nodded. It was obvious Omar was not going to let us hang around and harass Kaneesha any longer so we decided to go peacefully.

"I'll be checking my mailbox," said Rudy.

I shook my head at Omar, who shrugged with a *What do you want from me?* look on his face.

As we rode down the elevator together, Rudy and I decided to go grab a beer. We were parked on different levels and agreed to meet at Barney's Beanery to try to wash the bad taste of Pays Lee out of our mouths.

"Well, that's it. That motherfucker calls me again, I ain't answering the phone," said Rudy in between slugs of beer.

"Damn straight. I'm tired of his bullshit," I replied.

I asked Rudy how much Pays was into him and he said over fourteen grand. That was almost three times what he owed me.

Seems Rudy did a lot more 'round town stuff for Pays when he wanted to be incognito, driving him to backdoor meetings with white corporate executives who didn't want to be associated with the gangsta entourage but knew a good investment when they saw it. I explained my situation and told him Pays had me do his Vegas pick-ups because I was packing. He usually— though not lately—came back from Vegas with a satchel full of cash. Rudy didn't have a gun permit, and as far as I knew, didn't carry a piece. I explained that Pays was usually pretty good about paying C.O.D., but lately he'd been making excuses. Rudy confirmed that he thought Pays was being cut off by his backers but didn't know why since he was still producing hit after hit. We figured that maybe Pays' trips to Vegas had something to do with it, maybe losing big at the tables. Or maybe he was living too extravagantly, way beyond his means. Like with his private charter jet shuttling him back and forth.

We drank and commiserated about the stupid stuff Pays had us do for him, stuff that was no big deal when you're paid in cash but pissed you off when you weren't. Rudy told me about runs to Roscoe's to pick up chicken and waffles for Pays and his boys. I told Rudy about the night before with Lauren and how Pays dumped her on me, and who I thought she was. I left out the part about still having her purse and phone.

"Shit! Pichter is *his* lawyer! I've driven him to see him. Why didn't you bring that up in the office?" Rudy asked. "You could have told Omar she was still at your place or something. Pays would have freaked out."

"Rudy, he didn't give a shit about her, or who she is," I replied. "He had her sucking his dick in my back seat. He even offered her to me."

"You didn't..."

"Of course not!"

"Maybe he doesn't know who she is," he said. "As far as he's concerned, she's just some rap groupie. That would freak him out even more."

I mulled that over and wondered if it could be true.

"Well, maybe it's not too late to use that," I said.

"Maybe we should drop a dime on Pichter, tell him whose dick his stepdaughter's been sucking?" Rudy smiled.

"We do that we'll never get paid. Plus, our names will be mud."

People, particularly "known people" in Hollywood like their privacy. Rudy and I—and pretty much everyone below the line—have an unwritten, unspoken sort of oath not to reveal anyone's dirty laundry. And there's plenty of it. If someone hires you, and you ever want to work again, then you're expected to keep your mouth shut without having to be told to keep your mouth shut. Oh, rumors fly around, and sometimes TMZ or the paparazzi will get an anonymous tip now and then. But if you're going to spill the beans on someone, you better be getting a retirement fund. Because being below the line and talking dirt in Hollywood is career suicide.

I remember once when I was driving Gabriella. She was dating French flavor-of-the-month actor Jules Pinchot, and he had spent the day on the set watching Gabby work. As far as I was concerned, he was a frog, a Euro-trash asshole, but I couldn't say that to Gabriella. I drove them both around for a couple of days and on one occasion I dropped Gabby off at home and he came along for the ride. She had an early call the next morning so I was to take him back to the Chateau Marmot where he was staying. Instead he made a call on his cell phone and had me swing by the Viper Room on Sunset. When we arrived we picked up some strung-out Euro-trash fashion model that was waiting outside. When she got in the car, Jules broke out some blow and they started to snort. All I could think was if this guy leads Gabby down that broken path again, I'd wring his froggy neck.

When I dropped him off at the Chateau, Frenchy-boy told—not asked—me to wait. He'd be down in a bit and would need a ride back to the Viper Room. All of a sudden he thought I was his personal chauffeur. I watched him in the rearview as he got out of the car with Euro-chick. As soon as they entered the hotel, I turned the Suburban around and left. Who the fuck did this little shit think I was that I was going to wait around for him when all I was instructed to do was to give him a ride back to his hotel?

The next day I didn't mention anything to Gabby, as much as I wanted to. Had she asked, I would have told her everything but, again, part of my job was keeping people's secrets secret. Later that day he was on the set again, and after a long day of shooting, I drove the two of them to Spago for dinner. On the way back to Gabby's house afterward, they were in the backseat getting cozy. Jules started putting the moves on her. At first she seemed interested but then I noticed her push him away as he tried to round the bases. I heard her repeatedly say, "No." Finally, she told him to "Stop!" and when he didn't, I pulled the Suburban off the 101 and ducked down one of the quiet dark streets in the Woodland Hills area. Gabby, angry now, shouted, "Jules, stop it!" once more and that was all I needed. I pulled over, jumped out, and threw open the rear door. Jules was on top of her, groping and struggling against her to get his hand up her skirt.

He turned and looked at me and said, "Get back up there where you belong."

I dragged Frenchy out by the scruff of his neck and laid him down on the pavement. I got on top of him with my knee on his chest, pulled out my .45, and shoved it in his face.

"The lady said stop," I told him.

Like any chicken-shit Frenchman facing a gun, he quickly retreated into a whimpering fool, begging me not to kill him.

"Mike!" Gabby gasped from behind me.

I had no intention of killing him, but I wanted him to know he had crossed the line with Gabriella Vassey, and his life was now on the line because of it.

"Tell the lady you're sorry and that you won't be able to see her anymore," I told him.

"Who do you think you…?" he said before I backhanded bitch-slapped him then dug the barrel of my gun under his chin.

"I said, tell the lady you're sorry and that you won't be able to see her anymore," I explained again, jabbing the gun forcefully for emphasis.

"I'm…sorry, Gabby, but I won't be able to see you anymore," he said.

With that I got up, turned to Gabby who was watching wide-eyed, half-shocked but in a good way by what I had done.

"I'll take you home now," I told her as I closed the back door. I holstered my pistol and got back in the driver seat.

Frenchy was up, and as he reached for the door, I hit the electric door lock.

"What are you doing? Open the door! You can't just leave me here."

"Oh, no? Watch me." I closed my door and drove off. Frenchy boy tried in vain to chase us on foot but gave up after a few yards.

"Is this a safe place to leave him?" Gabby asked watching him disappear out the rear window.

"I suppose. As long as the coyotes don't get him," I said, winking at her in the rearview mirror.

Gabriella leaned forward on the front seat and touched my arm. "Thank you, Mike," was all she said. That was enough.

"You okay?" I asked. I could tell she was shaken up. She looked back at me and nodded.

When I dropped her off at her place, I walked her to her door. I told her about the night before with Jules, the Viper Room, the Euro fashion model, and the coke. I told her I was sorry and what I thought of Frenchy and that she was better off without him. She nodded.

"You're right. I don't know what I was thinking," she said.

As she opened her front door she turned and asked, "Would you have shot him?"

"No…unless I had to."

Below the line shooting above the line? No way. That would not only be career suicide, it would mean a life in the pen. I told her I'd never in my life pointed a gun at anyone before. Nor did I ever see anyone wet themselves.

Her eyes widened, and she asked, "Did he?"

I smiled and nodded. Gabby laughed, threw her arms around me, and kissed me on the cheek.

"Thank you," she whispered in my ear.

I smiled and said, "Seeya in the morning."

"Seeya in the morning."

Needless to say, that story never went any further than the three of us, and it was never mentioned again. Gabby didn't want any scandal, and I'm sure Frenchy didn't want word getting out either. In fact, he flew to London two days later to meet with a British director about the leading role in a film he was casting. When Jules found out Gabby was already cast as the female lead, he backed out due to "creative differences."

So if you're in the line of work that I'm in and you come across any inside dirt, it's got to be so scandalously juicy to garner such a high price that you won't need to or care about working anymore. Right now I couldn't see how this bit of information about Pays and Michelle Bartley's love child/Pichter's stepdaughter could provide that. We could probably bury Pays with it if anyone believed me, especially Pichter. But what would that get me? A one-way ticket to Palookaville, as they say.

"Our names won't be mud," Rudy said after a few more sips of his beer. "Pichter wouldn't want that word getting out. He'd take it out of Pays' hide."

I thought about that while we ordered another round and a couple of bowls of the second-best chili in Los Angeles.

"Well, it's not a bad idea. But I think we should give it a little time and see if he actually comes up with our money," I suggested.

"Sure, sure, of course. I'm just saying if he doesn't, we gotta have a plan to get some leverage on that fucker," Rudy said.

I thought about it, absently nodding. Rudy held up his new bottle for a toast and we clinked, each taking a long pull after.

CHAPTER 6

We called it a night probably later than we should have. By the time I got back to the marina, it was close to ten. Since I had to get up around 3:30 a.m., this didn't leave me too much time for sleep. I brought Lauren's bag inside with me and started to explore her smart phone. I checked out her phone book, and sure enough, there were numbers for Pichter, both professional and private.

I sat up when I got to her photos. They started out with innocent selfies of the attractive Lauren smiling at the camera, school friends, and a Yorkshire terrier. Then I came across shots of what appeared to be an exclusive hotel suite with the Las Vegas strip laid out below seen through the large picture window. Then came a couple of shots of Pays Lee pouring champagne, mugging it up, and toasting the camera. The next ones caught me off guard. They were graphic pictures of a naked Lauren in various, hard-core sexual poses. Some were of Lauren performing fellatio on a large black member. As I scrolled through more photos, sure enough, the recipient was Pays Lee. And it was obvious from the POV of photo angles into a large bedroom mirror that it was Pays who took all these shots. The clincher was a short, shaky video clip. Pays was pounding her from behind aiming the phone at the mirror while a naked Lauren screamed in pain or pleasure or both. Now, I'm certainly no prude when it comes to homemade pornography, but I was pretty taken back by this. Discovering Pays Lee was such a slime-bag, taking advantage of such a young girl, well, it really bothered me.

I wasn't sure what to do but before I called it a night, I had an idea. I realized I needed to have some insurance so I turned on my laptop computer, plugged the phone in, and downloaded the images. I wanted to return Lauren's bag and phone somehow, so I needed to copy this stuff. I have to say it made me feel sleazy—I wanted some leverage on Pays Lee, if I needed it, but I didn't really want this stuff on my computer. Instead, I decided to copy it straight to a thumb drive I remembered I had laying around. Some struggling screenwriter I met at the Hinano Bar had given it to me with his screenplay on it when I told him I was in the movie business. He used the thumb drive as his business card, and it had his name, Al Phillips, imprinted on it along with his phone number. He was drunk and rambled on about what a great movie it was going to make, and he wouldn't listen to a thing I said about how I couldn't help him. He insisted I take his thumb drive and give his screenplay a read. He said he was a screenwriter but really wanted to direct. I laughed—doesn't everyone? I had been dressed sharply and had a wad of cash on me, having just finished an airport pick-up. He probably thought I was above the line and could help him.

After downloading the images and the video, I hid the thumb drive in my hollowed-out copy of *Moby Dick*. I had cut out the center of the pages years ago for a place to hide my cash. Sitting on a bookshelf with the other hardcovers, it blended right in. It served me particularly well when I was married to Sandy. I could stash my per diem money there so I always had some cash on hand that she couldn't get her hands on. Plus books are the last thing burglars would look to steal. They never struck me as literary types.

When I finally lay down in bed, my mind was racing. How could I use these pictures to my advantage with Pays Lee? And if I could, should I? I was torn. The images from the phone were popping in my head and were really starting to bother me. I didn't want to hurt Lauren any more than this scumbag already had. Did I threaten Pays Lee with them for the money he owes Rudy and me? That felt a lot like blackmail, and I didn't really see myself as a blackmailer. Or do I hand them over to Pichter and let him bring down his wrath on Pays Lee? Hell, if I really want to bury him, I could turn them over to the press. They'd have a field day with it. With all the stories of sexual harassment cases flying around Hollywood these days, the police would have to get involved. Either way, I felt like it had the potential to come back and bite me in the ass if things didn't go right. I thought it best to try and sleep on it, since I wasn't going to do anything until I had a plan. I just had to come up with that plan.

I woke up at 3:20 a.m., ten minutes before my alarm was due to go off, and I jumped out of bed. Early call times made me nervous about being late, so I tended to be early. My body clock always kicked in when I needed it to for a paycheck. Work had been slow and these couple of days' work were like a godsend, especially with not seeing anything from Pays Lee. I was hoping I could parlay this gig it into more days, or even the run of the show.

I jumped in the shower while the coffee brewed. As I was filling my thermos cup, I noticed Lauren's phone still sitting beside my laptop. I put it back in her bag and grabbed it, along with my coffee, before walking out the door. Once in the Suburban, I stashed the bag back under the seat where I'd found it. One way or another, I was going to get it back to Lauren.

When I got to the studio, I was issued a walkie-talkie and a twelve-passenger van. After getting a quick tour from Joey Beans, Chris DeLuca's right-hand man, I was off to the races shuttling crewmembers to Stage 3 from the off-site parking lot. I had transferred Molly's wardrobe loaners from the Suburban to the back of the van so I could return them when I saw her.

There were two of us, Freddie Carson and me, doing the parking lot shuttle runs. If all went well, we would be in perfectly alternated positions—one of us picking up at the lot, the other dropping off at Stage 3. We stayed in radio communication so we could keep to that plan as best we could. This way no one had to wait too long for a ride to the set, and we could fill up the vans with crew on each run.

The morning started off fine with mostly grips, juicers, and camera geeks, followed by art dogs and vanity (the make-up crew). On my third run, I was happy to see Molly and her assistant, Marie, waiting for the shuttle in the parking lot. Molly's long, wavy strawberry-blond locks looked luxuriously sexy as they caught the golden hour light of sunrise. She was bundled up in a sweater for the morning chill and had on a pair of yoga pants that showed off her incredible butt and shapely, long legs. I leaned out the window and told her to come ride shotgun. She leaned over and gave me a friendly kiss as she got in.

"I'm glad to see you got on the show, Mike," she said.

"Just day-playing right now," I replied.

I told her I had the clothes she loaned me in the back and that I didn't end up needing them. She grilled me as to why, but I explained that the bird had flown the coup before I had gotten back.

"Boy, you really have a way with women," she remarked playfully.

"The story of my life," I said.

"We'll have to see about that," she said flirtatiously.

"Don't say I didn't warn you."

I dropped the rest of the crew off at Stage 3 then drove Molly and Marie right to their trailer. I walked them out and gave back the loaners from the back of the van.

"Maybe I'll catch you at lunch. I'll save you a seat," Molly said.

"Thanks, but I'm low man on the totem pole. They'll probably feed me early so I can work through lunch."

"Well, you'll be around…" she said hopefully.

"Oh, yeah. I'll come by and bug you when I get some down time."

"Sounds good. Have a great day." She dove into her trailer and started sorting through racks of clothes.

"You too," I called out as my walkie was calling me.

When I got back into the van, I saw Molly's soon-to-be-ex, Jimmy, heading for her trailer. He stopped by the van when he saw me and shook my hand.

"Glad to see you here, Mike. Like old times," he said jovially.

"No shit. You have anything to do with this?" I asked thinking maybe he put in the word for me with Chris DeLuca.

"No, but I'll be happy to take credit for it."

"In that case, thanks. I could use the work."

"You available for the run of the show?" he asked.

"Sure. I don't have anything else on my plate right now."

"George decided he wants to do some more location days, and they upped Chris's budget. So who knows?"

"Put in a good word for me," I told him trying not to sound too desperate.

"You got it." He shook my hand again and then stuck a finger to his earpiece as he got a call on his walkie. "Copy that. Have him meet me by the wardrobe trailer," he answered into his clip-on mic. Jimmy waved as he headed into Molly's trailer.

I watched for a moment to see what kind of vibe I could pick up from the two of them, but I lost sight of him. I hadn't seen them together since I heard the news of their break-up. I was also unsure if or how hard I should pursue with Molly. The three of us went way back, and I didn't want any bad blood between any of us if I could help it.

Freddie called me on my radio and said he was about to leave the parking lot. I answered, "Copy that. On my way," and took off.

Rudy was driving a fueling stake bed so when call time had passed and the whole crew was on set, the extras put out to pasture at Stage 2, and all the frantic last-minute errand runs were done, I called Rudy for a top off. As I fueled up, we came up with a plan to play a gag on Chris DeLuca to bust his chops. After his previous inquiry about seeing if we could work together, which we found out he asked both of us, we figured we could get his blood pressure up a couple of notches by feigning a brawl. Rudy knew the prop master on the show and promised to get a breakaway bottle or something to make it look good. We conspired to do it right outside his office trailer at wrap. If we made enough noise for him to come out and see us, one of us would bust the bottle over the other's head the moment he came out.

I was thinking of telling Rudy about the Pays Lee's photos I'd found on Lauren's phone but I still wasn't sure how much I wanted to share just yet. I had to admit it was great seeing Rudy again and renewing our long-lost friendship but a lot of water had flowed under our bridges since the good old days, and I wasn't quite sure where we stood with each other. I decided to keep quiet for now and see how it played out. I was still trying to devise a plan for how and when to use the photos, and I needed to think it through before I got anyone else involved. I still had to get Lauren's bag and phone to Pichter somehow. I figured it was best to get rid of it as soon as I could, in case someone found me with it. I thought I could run it over to Pichter's office tonight after work. I was sure there would be some kind of drop box or night watchman to accept packages after hours.

As expected, Chris lunched me and most of his drivers early so we could work though everyone else's lunch break. I made a mental note to swing by Molly's trailer later in the afternoon when things calmed down. I noticed Chris didn't break Rudy and me at the same time. He was trying to keep our contact with each other to a minimum just in case. I knew Rudy and I could use that to our advantage when we sprung our little practical joke on him.

The rest of the day went smoothly, and I got to kick back for a while in the afternoon. When I did, I popped in to see Molly. She had some down time too, so we headed over to craft service to grab a cappuccino. We talked a bit and caught up. I could tell she was taking the break-up with Jimmy pretty hard, but she was putting on a brave face. Jimmy had moved out, so she was still living in their hillside house in Laurel Canyon. She was thinking of selling but hadn't had the chance to do much about it yet because work was keeping her so busy.

"There are too many memories there. I go home at night and cry looking at all we carved out together there," she said. "Everything reminds me..." She trailed off.

"Sounds to me like you should get out of there. I'm sure you can sell that place easy, and quickly, and for a real nice price," I encouraged.

"I know, I know. I've got a realtor coming out to look at it this weekend. Saturday. Shit, I've got to call her back. The trouble is, I love that house."

"It's a great place."

"But I can't live there now. And that really sucks!"

"Hey, you'll find something else. Something better. Something that'll be all yours," I tried to assure her.

"I guess," she said in an unconvinced way.

I felt bad for Molly. Here she was, letting her guard down, and now that brave face had turned into a funk. She was hurting, but I wasn't sure how much shoulder I should give her to cry on. I decided to try and cheer her up.

"So, you've got the realtor on Saturday. How about sailing on Sunday?" I offered.

"Really?" she said, excitement in her voice.

"Sure. Why not?"

We made our date, and for all intents and purposes, I really did just want to take her out to cheer her up. I knew it would do her good, like sailing does me good when the going gets tough. Once you're out on the water, nothing else matters. It's a vacation from life, stress, and reality, whether it's an afternoon, a weekend, or a week. This would be my gift to Molly.

We finished up our coffees before both our walkie-talkies started calling us. I walked Molly back to her trailer where my van was parked and told her I'd catch her later. She seemed a little more upbeat, and I couldn't tell if it was from my sailing invitation or having some work to do. Either way, I was happy to see her come out of her funk.

At wrap, Rudy and I set up our little prank. We got Joey Beans, Freddie, and a bunch of our other teamsters buddies involved, along with Jimmy and a few of his assistants. Jimmy even talked George Rossi and Kevin Scott, the producer, to come by to really freak Chris out. And because they came, so did every one of their minions, P.A.s, gophers, and ass-kissers. They all crowded around as we started arguing loudly right outside Chris's mini Streamline trailer. I shoved Rudy right into the trailer and the whole thing shook. Jimmy yelled, "What the hell's going on?!" It didn't take Chris five seconds to throw open the door to see me and Rudy in a shoving match in front of half the crew and big brass. His eyes wide in panic, Chris came right for us to break it up, but as he did, Rudy grabbed the strategically placed foam rubber two by four and smashed it over my head. Out of the corner of my eye, I could see Chris almost have a heart attack as I went down, until everyone started laughing and applauding. By now, an even bigger crowd of cast and crew had gathered and was laughing too. Even Molly and Marie were there. Chris looked around red-faced, and by time he looked back at me, I was sitting up on the ground laughing too.

"You motherfuckers," was all Chris could say before Rudy and I both put our arms around him in a mock smooch and group hug until he shoved us both off. Everybody had a good laugh as Chris ran back into his trailer shaking his head, embarrassed. He slammed the door then quickly reopened it, stuck his head out and shouted at Rudy and me, "You're both fired!"

This drew more laughs. The joke worked and it endeared us

to everyone who'd seen it. We were in, and I knew I'd now get as many days as I wanted on the show.

Afterwards, when the crowd died down and I finished up the last of my shuttle rounds, I went to see Chris in his trailer. He shook his head and smiled when he saw me.

"You got me good, you son of a bitch."

"What are friends for?" I replied.

"I'm going to get you back, you know."

That was just what I wanted to hear. It meant I'd be around for a while. Today had turned into a fourteen-hour day, and I was happy about the prospect of more. A couple of weeks of this, along with the free meals to lower my overhead, and I'd be back in fat city and out of the poor house.

"So I guess that means you want me back here tomorrow?" I asked.

"I was hoping you'd be available for the rest of the week. But after that little prank, I'm not so sure..."

"Hey, you know Rudy put me up to it," I smirked.

"Yeah, I'm sure he really twisted your arm."

"I'll clean off my plate for you," I cracked.

"Hell, I may need you for the rest of production. They decided to do more location shit instead of doing all green screen." Jimmy had been right.

"I'm down with that. I could use a little steady."

"I'll let you know for sure by the end of the week." He got up and we shook hands. "If you behave!"

"Yes, sir, copy that," I saluted.

"But watch your ass! Because I *will* get you back for today."

"Bring it on, big boy," I said as I headed out the door.

As dog-tired as I was after my first fourteen-hour day in a long time, it felt good to be working again. It was coming up on 6:00 p.m., and I figured I still had time to run over to Pichter, Loam, and Stein's office on Sunset. Somebody was bound to still be there to accept the package. I planned to pack up Lauren's bag and cell phone in a Cinelab box I'd picked up on a run, and address it to Pichter. I figured if it were packed in an industry box, it wouldn't arouse suspicion, as well as keep the trail off me. I had the box and some packing tape I borrowed from the art department with me as I drove the van to the lot to pick up my Suburban.

Mine was the last car in the parking lot. Such is the life of a Hollywood teamster—the first to come and the last to leave. I pulled up next to the Suburban, locked up the van, and with the box and packing tape in hand, I turned to the Suburban. No sooner did I open the door and begin to climb in when out of nowhere, someone grabbed me from behind and pulled me out.

"What the...?" I said. I turned to face them but was met with a hefty battering ram of a punch in the solar plexus that knocked the wind out of me. I went down hard and doubled up. Whoever it was reached over me and hit the electric locks on the Suburban unlocking all the doors. The man was a stocky white guy in khakis and a navy blue sport jacket, with a military crew cut. He began what appeared to be a very calculated search of my vehicle. I knew he was no ordinary hood. This guy had to be on somebody's payroll, somebody big. These guys don't work cheap.

I had barely gotten to all fours when he pulled out Lauren's bag and began rifling through it.

"Hey, I gotta return that," I struggled to get out.

"Yeah, right," before he delivered a fierce, swift kick to my ribs, hard enough to lift me off my hands and knees, and flip me over back on my back.

With that, he stormed off, bag in hand. Mission accomplished. I couldn't do anything but lie there until the pain subsided and I could catch my breath. In the distance, I heard a car door open and close, start up, and take off, but I didn't get a look at it. My Suburban was the only vehicle in the lot so he must have parked on the street. I managed to crawl over to the Suburban and use it get to my feet and climb in. My ribs were screaming, but I started it up and sat there trying to figure out my next move.

Who was this guy? was all I could think about. I'd seen plenty of his type at the shooting range and during competitions. Khakis and a sport coat, he had to be some big money's bodyguard, ex-military, maybe even black ops kind of dude. He certainly punched like one. Only Hollywood big money hires those types of elite ex-military types. Pichter, I wondered? Who else would track me down for the sole purpose of getting Lauren's bag? Someone else who knew about the photos and had a grudge against Pays Lee? Not likely, but Pichter soon would have a grudge against him, if and when he saw the pictures on her phone. Maybe I should have deleted them when I downloaded to my thumb drive. Now that Pichter had them, I didn't really have any leverage left with Pays. Maybe I could make the offer to Pichter to keep the photos from going public, but I didn't think I wanted to run that risk. I sure didn't want to run the risk of running into Khakis Sport Jacket again. These guys were out of my league. Oh well, I didn't think I was cut out to be a blackmailer anyway. I took solace in knowing that when Pichter sees the photos, Pays would probably get a more meaningful visit from Khakis Sport Jacket. Yeah, it was out of my hands now.

I was hurting like hell by the time I got home. I poured myself a shot of Patrón from the freezer and downed it to kill the pain. I poured a second and went to the bathroom to inspect my wounds. Khakis Sport Jacket was indeed a pro. No marks on the face and no serious internal injuries as far as I could tell. I took my shirt off, and I could see the right side of my rib cage was sporting a nasty-looking welt that was turning from black and blue to a few other colors in the rainbow. It was tender to the touch, so I popped three Advils and washed them down with my second shot of Patrón. I checked my alarm clock before I collapsed into bed. I passed out as soon as my head hit the pillow.

The next morning, the pain in my ribs seemed to have spread all over my body. My whole body felt sore. I felt like I had just played running back in the Super Bowl without any equipment.

I got in the shower and made it as hot as I could stand it, which loosened me up a little. I followed that with an ice-cold rinse that was better than a slap in the face to wake me up. Grabbing my coffee, I was out the door, hoping the day would go by fast so I could get horizontal again as soon as possible.

The day started off smoothly enough. I did my shuttle rounds in the morning then ran a few errands for production and the sound department. I missed Molly in the morning, and she got on Freddie's shuttle. We did run into each other outside Stage 3 and traded greetings as they were getting ready to shoot a new scene.

When I saw Rudy later for a van top off, he said, "Hey, I got an idea—remember the other night when you told me about Jonathan Pichter and Michelle Bartley's daughter?"

"Forget it," I told him.

"No, listen. What if we call Pays and tell him you got a message from Pichter. He wants to know who his daughter was with over the weekend and how you ended up with her. You just ask Pays what he wants you to tell him. If Pays doesn't know who Pichter's daughter is and you tell him it was the bimbo he dumped on you, then he's probably going to freak out and want you to keep quiet. Then you can remind him of the money he owes us."

"Us?" I said.

"Yeah, us. Come on, I'm in deeper than you."

I thought about Rudy's plan but there were some holes in it. "First of all, Pays ain't gonna take my call. You know that," I pointed out.

"So you leave a message saying you got a call from Jonathan Pichter asking where you picked up his daughter."

"What if he knows she's Pichter and Bartley's daughter and doesn't give a shit?" I retorted.

"Oh, he'll give a shit. Believe me. Even if he knows, he won't want you ratting him out to Pichter. He's scared of Mister Big. I know, I've seen it. Pichter's got a lot of money invested in Pays.

And a lot of his friends invested in him too. Pays won't want to risk losing that. Not to mention what he could do to him career-wise. He could jack Pays up so bad even his momma wouldn't return his calls."

I shook my head.

"I can't do it, Rudy. Besides, Pichter may already know."

"What do you mean?" he asked.

I told him about what happened with Khakis Sport Jacket. The only thing I held back was the copies I had on the thumb drive. At this point, I didn't want anyone to know I had them. To drive the point home, I pulled up my shirt and showed him my rainbow bruise.

"Holy shit! You really think he was one of Pichter's guys?" He inspected the bruise, dumbfounded.

"I don't know, and I don't care. I'm done. Unless Pays decides out of the goodness of his heart to finally pay me, I'm just gonna write his invoice off as a loss. I do *not* want to fuck with the likes of Khakis Sport Jacket again."

"Yeah, I don't blame you, man. Hell, Pays may be up shit's creek if Pichter sees those pictures. Looks like I may have to write mine off as well. And that plain sucks. Because I cannot afford to lose all that."

"Well, it was a good run while it lasted. The Pays Lee express. Just have to find another money train like that," I added.

"Yeah..." Rudy leaned in. "I've been trying to work George Rossi. Maybe we can tag team him."

"He goes to Vegas a lot?"

"He goes all over. He's connected to the Hollywood gay mafia thing. He's ripe for a shakedown. Fucking around with all the young pretty boys...naked hot-tub parties, spiking the Snapple, circle jerk sleepovers...all that gay shit."

"Uh, great, but I think I'll pass. You can have it," I replied, shaking my head. I must admit that I was somewhat amused that Rudy still had a felonious streak in him. In the old days, back in The Bronx, we all had a touch of larceny in us.

CHAPTER 7

The rest of the week went by without a hitch. I fell into a rhythm working on the Rossi film, and the crew was starting to meld into a tight working unit. Of course, I couldn't look at Rossi the same way again having heard Rudy's dirty laundry about him but luckily I had little to no contact with him.

The stunt we played on Chris made Rudy and me mini-celebrities on the set. Everyone knew who we were. It paid off big time when Chris informed me he did want to keep me on for the run of the show. My ribs still felt stiff and sore, but they were getting better each day.

I kept checking my mailbox for a check from Pays Lee but no such luck. Saturday came, and I was finally able to sleep in after a sixteen-hour Friday spent packing up base camp to be ready to roll on location Monday morning. Stiff and sore, I'd popped another couple of Advils with a shot of Patrón and hit the sack. I slept till seven and it felt glorious. I figured I would clean *Stella* up so it would look presentable for Molly when she showed up the next day. Scrubbing down *Stella*'s deck was a chore with my sore ribs, but I worked through it knowing it would be a short day. While hosing her off, I got a call from that same no-show prospective buyer the week before. I told him the boat was sold. I did not need some asshole yanking my chain now that I had a steady gig for the next month, my slip fees were paid up, and I had a hot lady to take sailing. As soon as I hung up, I called Corey and told him to take it off the market.

I was fairly confident Molly would like sailing. Some women love it, some get seasick. Some are too prissy and never want to go out again. I knew Molly was different. She had that adventurous, down-to-earth outdoor streak that I really admire in a woman and was a rare thing in Hollywood. Molly wasn't the type who was afraid to get her hands dirty. She wasn't a bit like those Hollywood bimbo prima donnas who just want to be pampered and have everything done for them. She wasn't like that at all. I'd seen Molly work. Even in her home life—I'd seen her transform that little beat-up bungalow in Laurel Canyon into a swanky Hollywood Hills home with little help from Jimmy, other than his paycheck. It was Molly who had the vision, the gumption, and the elbow grease to get it done. And she did an amazing job. I was looking forward to showing her the sailing ropes, and seeing more of those freckles.

Since I hadn't received a paycheck yet, I was getting ready for a quiet Saturday night with a six-pack, some take-out, and maybe a movie on TV when the phone rang.

"Yo, Mikey, I need a pick up." It was Pays Lee.

I couldn't believe my ears. I decided to give him a hard time.

"Who is this?" I replied.

"Ah-ha, you funny, dude. Listen, I got your money. Cash. I'll pay you in full tonight when I get in."

I was trying to think of how I should play this. I wondered if he had already received the wrath of Pichter and possibly run into Khakis Sport Jacket—or was running from him. If so, I definitely didn't want any part.

"Pays, I'm booked up tonight. I suggest you call Carlisle."

Carlisle was a big Hollywood Limousine service catering to the entertainment industry.

"Carlisle? Shit! Get yourself unbooked, and meet me at ten."

I didn't like the way Pays was ordering me around, so it made it much easier for me to say, "No can do, Mister Lee. I got me a paying customer."

"Shit, Mikey, how much have I paid you in the last couple of years? I told you I'm gonna square up my debt tonight. Cash money! Imma text you a picture of it. So be at the airport at ten!" With that he hung up.

I was ready to go back to my lo mein and crack my second beer when my phone alerted me to a text. It was from Pays Lee. The body of the message was a selfie of a smiling Pays Lee holding up a small, red-leather designer duffle bag full of bank-bundled Benjamin greenbacks next to his smiling face, with the message, "C U @ 10."

Okay, I thought, now he's speaking my language. Maybe I could collect on my debt. As I thought it over, I considered calling Rudy to see if Pays had called him. Pays might pay the smaller amount he owed me but might not want not to pay the fourteen grand he owed Rudy. By the looks of that picture, he certainly had it though. What the hell, I decided to call Rudy anyway. The phone rang a bunch of times before going to voicemail.

"Hey Rudy, it's me. You'll never guess who just called wanting a pick-up tonight. Call me and I'll fill you in."

As I hung up, I started to wonder if this could be some kind of set-up. If Pichter was giving him holy hell then maybe Pays would be looking for some payback. If so, having Rudy there for a backup wasn't a bad idea. But the more I thought about it, I figured why would Pays Lee think I had anything to do with what Pichter found on Lauren's phone? I didn't, after all. All I did was see what was on it before Khakis Sport Jacket spontaneously obtained it from me.

As I dressed for the Pays Lee pick-up, I decided that besides my normal carry—a compact 1911 .45—I would strap on my ankle-holstered compact .38. Pays knew about (and wanted) me carrying the .45 for his protection, but the .38 would be *my* protection, in case he was out to fuck me up. Loading my pockets with my wallet and keys, I grabbed my folding knife and stuck it in as well.

I chose to arrive a bit late. Pays was usually on time, so I thought I'd make him sweat a bit since he made me sweat about getting paid. If he was in fact holding all that cash, it would make him all the more nervous.

At 10:10 p.m. I drove through the Cloverfield gate and onto the tarmac, heading toward the charter's hangar. As I approached, a black Dodge Charger with dark tinted windows roared by me in the opposite direction. I tried to think who that could be, but I didn't know any of Pays' crew who had a black Charger. Up ahead, I could see the jet right outside the open hangar door. I pulled closer, and the light from inside the hangar silhouetted a few heaps of baggage on the ground near the jet. I got closer and hit them with my headlights—the heaps weren't bags at all. One of them was a pile of blue paisley laying in a growing puddle of blood.

I drove up as close as I could and pulled out my .45. I held it ready as I got out of the Suburban and approached the scene. Sure enough, there lying on the ground was Pays Lee. Coming closer, I could see bullet holes in his chest and half his skull blown apart. I felt my lo mein coming up and had to swallow down the bile to keep from hurling. A few yards away was Omar, the second huge heap on the ground. His eyes were wide open, his mouth open, full of blood and his hands in a death grip on his bloody neck where he'd been shot. I looked around, scanning the area, with my pistol pointed in case the killer was still around. Then I remembered that black Charger racing away and figured that must have been the shooter, or shooters. I didn't see any of the flight crew and guessed they were either dead on the plane or they left before the shooting started.

I was trying to wrap my brain around what to do and instinctively pulled my out my phone and dialed 911. But then I saw it—the red-leather duffle bag, still slung over Pays' shoulder, his hands clutching it.

"Nine-one-one, what is your emergency?" said the operator. As I tiptoed closer she repeated, "Nine-one-one, what is—"

I quickly hung up.

I had to think fast now that I had called 911. There would be a record of the call from my phone number. I holstered my .45 and approached cautiously, careful not to add anything to the "crime scene." I bent over and I tried to open the bag to see if the money was in fact inside. I unzipped a corner and saw the neatly packed bundles inside. It was still packed full.

I tried to act calm as I looked around, scanning the area once more to see if anyone was watching. There were a couple of camera globes hanging above the hangar door and walkway, but I figured those were focused on the doors themselves monitoring for anyone trying to gain entrance. I was mostly out or range and certainly blocked by the jet itself, if either camera was even pointed in my direction.

This was more cash than I'd ever seen at one time, probably more than I'd ever see again. Thinking I was alone and in the clear, I bent down, grabbed the bag, and pulled—but it wouldn't budge. The shoulder strap was around Pays, and he was half on top of the bag. My heart was pounding. I looked around once again. If I was ever going to see the money Pays Lee owed me, this was going to be it. So I grabbed the bag again, gave a hard pull and yanked, turning Pays over and twisting his gruesome corpse into a very unnatural position. In doing so, his brains—or what was left of them—spilled out of his half-missing skull. I gagged and swallowed. It was all I could do to keep from puking all over him. The damn strap was still wrapped around him. I yanked and pulled to no avail. Finally, I pulled out my folding knife and cut the strap. I pulled the short end out from under him, freeing the bag. I stepped back and opened the zipper wider. It was stuffed full of crisp, hundred-dollar denomination bank-wrapped bills. This was above-the-line money.

Zipping the bag closed, I quickly walked it back to the Suburban continuously looking around to see if anyone was around watching or witnessing me. On the other side of the runway, revelers were outside on the deck of Monsoon, the airport restaurant, hooting and hollering as a Cessna came in for a landing. The Saturday night music and crowd were loud over there so I doubt if anyone had heard the shooting. I was also betting none of them were taking any interest in me or notice of my Suburban.

I threw the bag in the way-back but when I closed the door, I noticed blood on my hands. I reopened the door and grabbed some baby wipes I kept in the back and cleaned myself up. I saw the bag had blood on it as well. It was hard to tell on the red leather in the darkness, but I figured I'd clean that up later. I had to get out of there, fast, and stash the bag somewhere.

I hopped in the driver's seat and threw it in gear. As I drove out, my head was spinning over what had just happened and what I had to do. Why didn't the person who shot Pays Lee take the money? Do I call the police? I should. I will. I had to. There was already had a record of my number calling 911. When? In this day and age, there had to be more cameras around, and I was sure I was on them. But what did they see? Me, arriving and leaving, no doubt. If somehow they saw me take the bag, I was royally fucked. But I was pretty confident and betting they didn't. This was a big payday, and I was willing to play the odds. The police would be talking with me, eventually. I knew that. I figured I could feign fear and panic as the reasons why I left the scene—and not so far from the truth. In the meantime, I had to hide this bag.

I pulled out of the Cloverfield gate, and as I did, I noticed a black Charger parked in the industrial park off Ocean Park all by itself. As I slowed to check it out, the headlights flashed on, and *bang!* A loud report hit my passenger side window directly between the Charger and me. Had it not been for the bulletproof window, I would have taken it right between the eyes. I stomped on the gas and turned west on Ocean Park. The Charger burned rubber and followed. I floored it and barely beat a yellow light turning red. In my rearview, the Charger barely slowed and blew right through the light. I weaved in and out of the light evening traffic until I saw an opening. I made a sharp left turn on a southbound street, and took the first right into an alley. Flying down the alley, I kept my eyes glued to the rearview. When I got to the end of the alley, I saw the Charger enter. I flew right again, then another quick right north on Ocean Park. There were several cars parked in front of the Moose Lodge and saw my opening in front of a van. I whipped into the spot and killed the lights, eyes on my side-view mirror to see which way the Charger would go. As I waited, I pulled out my .45 and clicked off the safety.

I saw the Charger nose out onto Ocean Park and hesitate. I breathed a sigh of relief as he went left and roared off. I waited until the Charger was well out of view before I holstered my gun, turned my lights back on and pulled out. I still had to get down to the marina to stash the bag. I took a zigzag route down side streets until I got to Walgrove, then shot down to Washington. I was hoping whoever was in the Charger didn't know who I was or where I lived but I kept a sharp eye out for him.

There was no sign of the Charger when I got back to Marina del Rey and I drove down Panay Way to the C Basin where Ari Goldman's boat was berthed. I hopped aboard, unlocked the cabin, and took the bag below. It was a fairly roomy cabin cruiser, especially compared to my sailboat. Last time I heard from its owner, he wasn't planning on being back in the states anytime soon. There was no paper trail connecting me with that boat, and it was the safest place I could think of hiding the bag at the moment, with the least likelihood of getting searched if the cops came looking for me.

In the captain's suite, I flipped up the mattress and opened a storage locker beneath the bunk. I opened the bag, turned it over, and emptied the money into the storage compartment. I was taken back by the amount of bundled cash that fell out, way more than I expected. I picked up one of the bundles of hundreds and looked at the band: ten thousand dollars. I didn't know how much was there or how many bundles, but it was hundreds of thousands of dollars, at least. After putting the mattress back and locking up the boat, I walked the bag out to the end of the dock. I knelt down and stuck the bag in the water letting it fill up. When it felt heavy enough I gave it a hefty toss out into the middle of the basin and watched it sink. As I walked back to the dock, I glanced once more at the Ari's boat and realized how fitting its name was: *Above the Line*.

After washing up and flushing the bloody baby wipes down the toilet in the dockside bathroom, I drove back about halfway to the airport and pulled into a British pub I knew of on Lincoln Boulevard. From the parking lot, I dialed 911 once more. Checking my watch it had been about thirty-five minutes since I left the airport. I figured I could make a plausible story out of that.

"I'd like to report a shooting," I said trying to sound as panicked as I could, which wasn't too hard.

After filling in the dispatcher on the whats, the wheres, the whens, and the whos, she told me to remain where I was until the police arrived. As soon as I hung up, I ran inside and ordered a shot of Jack, threw it back, and immediately ordered another. The police arrived about ten minutes later. By then I was nursing a pint of Newcastle and my nerves were settling. My story was coming together in my head. The chase with the Charger gave me the perfect excuse for not calling back sooner. But I had to come up with a viable excuse for leaving the scene initially. I figured I could play the panicked limo driver since it wasn't too far from the truth.

The uniformed cops who came to pick me up informed me that the police had already received another call about the shooting and were on the scene at the airport. I wondered who made that call, but didn't ask. The uniforms who came to see me were assigned to pick me up and bring me back to the scene so that detectives could interview me. When I learned that, I gave very little to the uniforms so I wouldn't get tripped up on my story.

On the way to their patrol car, I suddenly remembered I was

still packing and offered this up to the officers before they could think I was keeping it from them. I handed over both my compact auto .45 and ankle-holstered .38, along with my concealed carry permit. They patted me down to make sure I didn't have anything else and took my folding knife. But I could tell the officers felt more at ease that I came clean about my firearms before they found out on their own. Maybe it would help endear me to the detectives as well? Having worked on *Beach Patrol*, I also knew a few Santa Monica police officers, even brass, who'd been assigned to the show as advisors. I was hoping they were still on the force since I planned on dropping their names if the right time came.

The uniformed cops unloaded and sniffed my guns to make sure they hadn't been fired recently. Thankfully I had decided to clean *Stella* instead of going to the range like I normally do on a Saturday morning. On the way to the airport in the back of the patrol car, I kept my answers to their questions short, brief, and vague. The cops already knew the victim was Pays Lee and being on this case was a big deal for them. One of their primary concerns was keeping the paparazzi at bay. I wasn't sure how much they knew about me while I was on the scene, and I didn't want offer anything too significant until I knew more. My talk with the detectives was going to be what really mattered, and I was still formulating that in my head in the patrol car on the way over.

When we arrived at the scene, it was in full-blown investigation mode. Bright work lights were being set up. Curtains had been raised around the bodies as the forensic team arrived and started photographing them. Little numbered triangles were laid about the ground, marking shell casings and other tiny bits of evidence. It was all being carefully analyzed and cataloged by crime scene technicians. I wondered if any of those little numbers marked anything to do with me, something I might have left behind. The scene looked very much like the movie sets I'd worked on except there were no cameras or assistant directors yelling, "Rolling, cut, reset." It all looked like a very serious, professional, and scientific operation.

I was led over to the lead detective and was surprised and relieved to see who it was. Detective Rick Gomez had moved up in the ranks. I knew him when he was a uniformed sergeant assigned to *Beach Patrol*. His was one of the names I was planning on dropping when I got here. It was always a cushy gig for any cop, getting assigned to movie or TV sets. It was not without its perks. These duties were usually left for retirees or about-to-be retirees. But Gomez was a young guy. He ran all the cops on set and was obviously well connected to have that assignment. We had gotten to know each other fairly well back in the day and I wondered if he would remember me. I shook his hand warmly and called him by his first name before he had a chance to introduce himself.

"Good to see you, Rick."

"It's Detective Gomez," he replied as he scrutinized me, trying to place me.

"Mike Millek," I offered. "Used to work on *Beach Patrol*."

He smiled at that. Back in the day, I had hooked him up by introducing him to some hot bikini extras that were into cops. I know for a fact he scored more than a couple of times.

"That was a long time ago. You drove the boat, right?" He remembered.

"Yeah. Congratulations on the promotion, Detective," I said, trying to butter him up.

"Thanks. It was a long time coming," he offered before getting down to business. "So, what can you tell me about all this, Mike?"

"Not too much. I was scheduled to pick up Pays, and when I got here, this is what I saw," I said nodding toward the scene.

I told him about the Dodge Charger that was leaving as I was arriving. I explained that I thought the bodies were bags tossed from the plane until I got a closer look. When I saw who it was, I panicked and took off, not knowing if the killer was still around. Then I told him about seeing the Charger again right outside the airport, and the shot fired at me. How I took off and the Charger gave chase. I elaborated a bit on that to fill up the time frame of me stashing the bag. Once I lost the Charger, I explained, my nerves got the better of me and I stopped for a stiff one while I called it in.

"You happen get a plate number?" he asked.

"No, I didn't. When I spotted the Charger, he flashed his brights, fired the shot and came right at me. It was all I could do to get away from him," I answered truthfully.

He seemed to be buying it, but then his senior, no-nonsense, Asian partner showed up, after conferring with the uniforms that picked me up. "What did the driver look like?" he asked.

"I didn't really see him," I replied.

"Then how did you know it was a him?"

I shrugged my shoulders, speechless. "I guess...I don't. I just assumed."

"Mike, my partner, Detective Lo," Gomez offered.

I reached out to shake his hand but he left me hanging. He was shorter than me but built solidly, hands on his hip and chest out. He was playing the macho cop card, trying to intimidate me. I let him think he was, to a point.

"Why did you leave the scene without calling the police?" he asked in an accusatory way.

"I started to, but I was kind of freaked out by the whole scene. I wanted to get away from here and call. But then the Charger shot at me and came after me."

Gomez jumped in saving me.

"Not an easy thing to get used to," he nodded toward the crime scene.

"I wouldn't think so," I concurred.

"Why were you carrying two pieces?" his partner asked.

"I always do when I work with this client," I lied. "He hangs around with some...shady characters, and I like to be...protected."

"What kind of shady characters?" he asked.

"Don't you know who that is? That's Pays Lee! He's one of the biggest gangsta rap producers in the business. It's not like he's hanging out with Boy Scouts."

I could tell Lo didn't like my answer, but that's what you get for asking stupid questions. Gomez jumped back in and regained control of the interview. We started going over the timeline, and I admitted I was running late for the pick-up.

Lo jumped in again at that point, "Pretty convenient, showing up late the day your client gets killed."

"Good chance I'd be laying there beside him if I hadn't," I replied.

"That's what I mean. Pretty convenient!" he shot back.

"You think I had something to do with this?" I shot back, indignant.

"You tell me." He stared me down.

I turned to Gomez. More to shut his partner up, I asked him flat out, "Am I going to need a lawyer?"

"No, Mike. You're not going to need a lawyer. We're just trying to piece things together here," said Gomez.

"Well, I'm happy to help out any way I can, but if I'm being accused of something..." I let drift off.

"Nobody's accusing you of anything, Mike."

"Not yet," muttered Lo.

I put my hands out in Lo's direction while I turned to Gomez with a WTF look on my face. He grabbed my arm and pulled me aside.

"Don't worry about him. Listen, would you mind coming down to headquarters so we can sort your story out and write up a statement?" he asked.

I finally figured out they were playing me: Good cop, bad cop. "Sure, no problem," I said, as innocently as I could.

I knew I'd be up half the night, answering the same questions over and over, confirming timelines to see if I would falter or change my story. But by this point, I was ready. I'd been through this before, growing up in The Bronx. I'd been interviewed by the police. Even if they had something on me, the rule on the street was you deny anything and everything, and never rat anyone out. Now I had no one to not to rat out, but I did have some denying to do to keep from turning over that cash. Cops are all pretty much cut from the same cloth no matter where you go. I figured if I could get one over on New York's Finest when I was fifteen after me and Rudy broke into the liquor store on Eastchester Road, these Santa Monica cabana boys would be a cakewalk.

As Gomez and Lo drove me to headquarters behind Santa Monica City Hall, I did my best to maintain my cool. In the back of my head, I was worrying about all the little details that could potentially be fatal to my story. I wondered about cameras I might not have seen or any evidence they might find that showed I grabbed the bag and ran. What if they test my knife and match fibers on Pays Lee? Did leather even have fibers? I knew it was crazy, but I was now also wondering why Rudy never called me back. Could he be a part of this?

I inquired about the plane crew and found out they had left the scene before the shooting. That made sense. Charter pilots and crew usually split as soon as they land and park. Lo asked if I owned any .40-caliber handguns, so I assumed that was the murder weapon, or at least the caliber of shell casings found at the scene. I told him I did not. His smart-aleck remark was that he could find out. I told him to go ahead.

"How many handguns do you have?" asked Gomez.

"A couple…"

"More than the couple you gave the officers?" Lo asked.

"Yeah. I also have a competition Colt 1911, a Smith & Wesson .357 N Frame, a .380 Walther PPK, and a Ruger Super Six .22."

"That's more than a couple," said Lo.

"Okay, a few," I corrected and added, "I compete with a lot of LAPD and sheriff's deputies. U.S. Pistol Shooting Association."

I didn't mention my shotguns or long arms. "Want to see my membership card?"

"That won't be necessary," said Gomez.

"You know Albert Molino?" I asked. I knew every law enforcement officer in L.A. County knew of Albert Molino. LAPD Officer Molino had shot a strung-out, meth-tweaking perp right between the eyes as he held a gun to a woman hostage's head. "He's a good friend of mine," I offered as a casual reference.

Gomez and Lo exchanged looks but kept on driving in silence.

When we got to headquarters, they put me in an interrogation room, presumably to sweat it out while they got updates from the other investigators at crime scene. Coming down from the adrenaline and Jack Daniels, I realized I'd be waiting a while, so I laid my head on the table, closed my eyes, and made like I was taking a snooze, in case anyone was watching me through the two-way mirror. About forty minutes later, Gomez and Lo noisily re-entered, so I "woke up" and rubbed my eyes as they sat down across from me. Gomez asked me if I wanted any coffee, and I said sure. He looked to Lo who got up and went for the door.

"Black, please," I called off to him as he went out the door.

Gomez had a yellow legal pad and was already writing. "So, Mike, did you happen to move anything, or take anything when you got to the crime scene that first time?"

"No, sir," I replied, deciding to add the "sir" as a sign of respect. "I was too freaked out. Why?"

"We're still trying to determine that," he said.

I figured Lo was probably behind the two-way mirror watching me for tells or any sign of deception while Gomez was directed his line of questioning.

"So you arrived at the scene at approximately 10:10 p.m.?" he asked, checking his notes.

"Yeah, I remember checking my watch because, like I told you, I was running late," I said.

"And you saw the bodies lying there just as they were?"

"Yes, sir."

"Then what?" he asked.

"Like I told you...I suddenly thought the shooter might still be in the hangar or nearby so I drew my gun and kind of...surveyed the area. I remember I instinctively pulled out my phone and dialed 911. But then I got a bit closer and saw Pays' head...the blood...I about lost it. I had to get out of there."

"So you hung up on 911?"

"I guess, I don't even remember. I must have," I said as convincingly as I could.

"Then what?"

"Uh, I hurried back to my car, got in, and headed out."

"So, what was your plan at this point? What were you going to do? Where were you going?" he asked.

"Plan? I didn't have a plan. I just wanted to get the hell out of there. I guess I was thinking I could probably pull over and park in that little industrial park to call back. But then the Charger was there and whoever was inside shot at me. I took off, and the Charger took off after me. I know now it was probably a dumb thing to do, but I wanted to get away from that hangar. The whole thing was freaking me out."

"Right. Freaking you out..." He scribbled as he spoke.

It went on like this for another ten minutes or so, and I tried to keep my cool before Lo finally came back in with the coffee. Which was, as I figured, the worse cup of coffee I'd ever tasted. I wondered if Lo spit in it.

Once Lo was back, the questions started getting repeated with minor elaborations, like I knew they would. I think I managed to keep it straight, stick to my story, and not let on too much more. After about the third or fourth go-round, they casually mentioned the bag to see how I would respond, no doubt.

"Where was the leather bag when you first saw the bodies?"

"What leather bag?" I asked with my best poker face.

Gomez feigned looking through his notes, "Didn't you

mention seeing a red leather duffle bag?" he asked again.

"No. Why would I?" I answered innocently.

Gomez was still checking his notes, as Lo was watched me like a hawk.

"I'm sorry, that was someone else," he told me.

Bullshit, was all I could think. So they knew about the bag. They could have gotten that from the flight crew, probably even knew its contents and that it was missing. They were trying to get me to sweat, but I managed to play dumb and cool, looking both of them straight in the eyes.

"Did Pays Lee usually carry large amounts of cash when you picked him up?" asked Lo.

"I have no idea. He usually paid me cash, but that was just a few hundred bucks. Not a lot of cash for a guy like him I would think," I pointed out.

"Why do you say that?" asked Gomez.

"Isn't the guy worth like...millions," I said, again, playing dumb.

"So you never saw him carrying bags full of money?" he followed up with.

I shrugged my shoulders. "He usually had a bag. What he had in the bag? I have no idea. He was usually coming from Vegas, so who knows? Could have been, I guess," I offered.

They yanked my chain for another couple of hours, going over and over my story and timeline. They finally confirmed they found a spent .40 shell casing in the industrial park lot. They had also sent someone out to get my Suburban and check out the bullet mark on the window, confirming my story. But they continued to question me about every detail. They were wearing me down, but I managed to keep to my story. Finally, around 3:30 a.m., I'd had enough.

"Hey, guys, can I go home now?" I asked.

"We just have a couple more questions," replied Gomez, and he went on to repeat questions I'd already answered. After another ten minutes of this, I got adamant.

"Look, we went through all this a bunch of times now. I'm tired and I want to go home. I want to help, but I've got nothing else to say. You want to keep me here, then arrest me and let me call my lawyer."

"No one's arresting you, Mike," said Gomez.

"Then I would like to go home...please."

Gomez and Lo exchanged looks and got up to leave.

"Okay, give us a minute," said Gomez, as he led a pissed off-looking Lo out the door.

I sat there and counted to myself. I got to three-hundred-forty-eight before the door opened again. It was Gomez.

"Okay, Mike, we're going to get a couple of uniforms to take you back to your car," he said.

"Thank you," I said as I got up and headed to the door.

We passed Lo in the hallway, and he gave me his cold, hard stare as I walked by. To get his goat, I smiled at him, thanked him for the coffee, and told him to have a good night.

"We'll be in touch, Millek," he said. He gave me the evil eye.

"You got my number," I replied. Fuck him, I thought.

When I asked about getting my guns back, Gomez informed me that they were going to run some forensic tests on them, and because it now was Sunday, they'd have to hold them for a few days.

"So am I a suspect?" I asked.

"It's routine. Whenever we have a shooting and there's a gun owner involved, we have to check it out."

I thought, *Bullshit! Fucking People's Republic of Santa Monica!* But I said, "I'd like a receipt for those, please."

Gomez tried to butter me up, thanking me for coming in and asking if I remembered anything else to give him a call, as he handed me his card. I gathered my stuff, snatched it out of his hand, and followed the uniforms out to their black and white.

My Suburban was now at police headquarters. It looked like it had been dusted for prints, and there was some kind of residue on the window around the bullet mark. I was curious if they found any blood around the back door but I didn't want to look since Gomez was watching me leave.

By time I got home, it was coming up on 5:00 a.m. Molly was coming at 10:00 a.m. to go sailing. I set my alarm for 9:30 a.m. and tried to get some sleep. I was dog-tired, my ribs were aching, and had a million things running through my head. Most of all, the cash I stashed on Ari Goldman's boat. I wanted to go get it, to see how much there was, but I knew I didn't dare go near it right now.

CHAPTER 8

The alarm woke me up, but the only thing that got me out of bed was the thought of sailing with Molly. I jumped in the shower while the coffee brewed, and I went over everything that had transpired the night before. I thought again about the cash, but I still didn't want go near it. As I drank my first cup, I loaded up the sailing cooler with some goodies, beer, cheese, fruit, chips and a salsa I had bought the day before, and a can of stuffed grape leaves I found in my kitchen cabinet. I had given Molly the slip number and she was waiting by the gate when I got there.

"'Morning, Captain!" she greeted me.

"Sorry I'm late," I said and gave Molly a hug and a peck in the cheek. "I had a very late night."

Molly looked great as usual, dressed casually in a white button-down shirt opened to her freckled cleavage and tied at the waist. She wore capri pants that she filled nicely and had a tote bag over her shoulder with the additional layers I suggested she bring. "Hanging out with those young girls again?"

"Actually I was at the Santa Monica police station getting questioned about the murder of a client I was supposed to pick up," I said.

She looked at me quizzically, not sure if I was kidding or not. "Are you serious?"

"Yeah, really. I'll tell you all about it as we head out," I said.

I unlocked the dock gate and led the way to *Stella*.

I helped her get aboard and she had a look around on deck. "It's nice." She smiled.

"Thanks. She's a little long in the tooth, but she sails like a lady," I replied.

Molly noticed the name and asked, "Who's Stella?"

"The previous owner's wife. Her nickname."

"You're okay with your boat having the name of somebody else's wife?"

"It's bad luck to change a boat's name. Besides, I had an aunt named Stella I was really fond of when I was a kid. She always tried to spoil me. I like to think it's a tribute to her."

While I ran the blowers and fired the engine to warm up, I unlocked the companionway and showed Molly around below, where to put her stuff, how to use the head, the basics. After all the food, drinks, and gear were stowed, I tossed off the dock lines and backed her out into the basin. Molly took to things quickly. She seemed comfortable, offered her assistance coiling dock lines and acting as lookout on the foredeck as we got out to the main channel. I asked her to take the helm while I went to the mast and raised the mainsail. She took it with no problem and followed the heading I gave her. We were heading directly into the wind, and the mainsail flapped noisily in the breeze. I fell back into the cockpit and asked Molly if she was okay steering. She wore a big smile and said, "No problem." I could tell she was getting the sailing bug already. I explained basic sailing to her, allowing her gain a feel of it, then let her turn into the sailing lane.

I threw the engine into neutral, and as we turned, the stiff breeze caught the mainsail and heeled the boat over a bit. She got a bit startled but recovered quickly and went with it, getting her sea legs. I explained falling off the wind and heading up, and I let her experience both while she was at the wheel. When we got to the far side of the sailing lane, I told her, "Helm's alee," and she turned the boat through the wind and fell on a port tack while I trimmed the mainsail. She got a kick out of that, and I could tell she was already starting to enjoy herself.

We tacked back and forth a couple more times until we got to the north exit of the main channel and headed out to the open bay. The wind and swell picked up as we cleared the breakwater and I talked her through the other boat traffic around the entrance. When we finally had some sea room, I told Molly to head up into the wind as I unfurled the jib foresail. As soon as I pulled it out from the forestay, I told Molly to fall off and gave her a target of a Santa Monica mountaintop off the pier to aim for. The jib filled with the wind as I trimmed the sails. *Stella* took off like a trotting thoroughbred out for a Sunday jaunt after being cooped up in the corral all week. I trimmed the sails so we wouldn't heel too much but still made the most of the nice ten-knot breeze. Once on course, I killed the engine and threw the transmission in reverse to kill the whirring sound of the engineless prop spinning in the water.

I always saw this moment as special, when your sails are on trim and you kill the engine. All the noise dies away, and it's suddenly just the wind in the sails and the sound of the water flowing by the hull. Sailing magic.

"Now," I said, "we're sailing."

Molly beamed. "This is wonderful!"

I was happy to see she was enjoying it so much. Somehow I knew she would. I didn't want to make her feel obligated to stay at the wheel and offered to take over.

"I should probably put on some sunscreen," she said.

I agreed and jumped up to take the helm from her while she headed below. As she stood in the companionway applying sunscreen to her face and cleavage, she asked me about the night before. I told her that Pays Lee was one of my regular clients and what I saw when I went to pick him up.

"That rapper guy? It was all over the news this morning!"

"That doesn't surprise me."

"So you were the one that found his body?" she asked.

I nodded.

"Oh my god, Mike, why didn't you call me? We could have rescheduled."

"Why? I've been looking forward for this all week," I told her.

"Me too." She smiled. "But that must have been...traumatic?"

"Not as traumatic as getting chased by the killer," I threw in.

"What?! Are you serious?"

"Yeah, he took a shot at me. Thank God the windows on my Suburban are bullet-proof." I told her about the Charger and the chase and how I eventually lost him. She came back up, sat next to me in the cockpit, and questioned me until I had pretty much told her the whole story. Everything except about the bag and the money.

"Are you okay?" she asked, looking me in the eye and taking my hand.

"I think so. A lot better now that I'm out on the water...and with you." I smiled.

We shared a moment looking in each other's eyes until she looked off around us.

"This is really beautiful. I can't believe how fast we're moving just on wind power." She pointed into the distance. "Is that Catalina? Can we go there?"

It was a clear day and one of the times you could actually see Santa Catalina Island from the bay.

"We could, but it would take us all day. We might not make it back in time for call tomorrow."

"Too bad."

"Maybe some other time. We can make a weekend out of it," I offered.

"Yeah." She smiled, turned, and leaned back against me. I put my free arm around her.

"This is really nice," she said and took my hand.

We sailed north up the coast past the Santa Monica Pier. Molly got a big kick out of seeing the seals lounging on the

Santa Monica buoy. Still leaning on me, she put her legs up on the bench, and I tried not to move to keep her comfortable. My ribs were aching but it felt good having her close. Ever since Sandy, I'd sworn I'd never get too involved with another woman. I did not want to go through that heartbreak again. Every woman I'd been with since had strictly been for a good time. When things started getting too close, or too clingy, I'd break things off and find someone else. Not too hard to do in the business I was in. There was always a new horizon to explore or someone waiting in the wings. But it had been a while since I had close contact with any woman, and Molly reminded me of what I was missing. Her hair smelled wonderful, and I nuzzled it affectionately, taking it in. I could have stayed like this all day, but it was time to tack because we were heading toward to the beach and about to lose our wind.

"Time to come about," I said.

Molly sat up and I asked her to take the helm, while I handled the sheets. We switched positions and when I was ready I turned to her and nodded.

"Helm's alee," she said and turned the wheel through the wind. I waited until the jib luffed and let the starboard sheet loose, while I pulled in the port sheet. I trimmed the jib sheet and then the main for a beam reach as we headed straight out to sea away from the shoreline. We stayed on this course, passing a couple of other sailboats heading north, perpendicular to us. Once out in the clear with some sea room around us, I asked if she was okay with the helm while I gathered some snacks. The sun was out in full now, and on this tack it got a lot warmer. I broke out a couple of Coronas and passed one up to Molly while I prepared our little feast. When I had everything ready, I rigged up my homemade gimbaled table that I attach to the steering column. After I set everything out, I took the helm, back-winded the jib, and locked the wheel so we were hove to. Molly and I sat, clinked bottles, and dug in. She asked about the heaving to, and I said it was a way of kind of braking the boat in the middle of the ocean.

"Why don't you just drop the anchor?" she asked, pointing to the pulpit where my Danforth anchor was rigged.

I explained that where we were was way too deep to anchor. According to the depth gauge, we were in almost two hundred feet of water. Even though I had three hundred feet of anchor rode, it was not enough to anchor safely. Anchoring required at least a four or five-to-one ratio of depth to anchor line. Meaning, if you were in twenty feet of water you needed to let out about eighty to a hundred feet of anchor line, or rode as it's called, which included the twenty to forty feet of chain attached directly to the anchor. The theory behind anchoring was that the weight of the chain would keep the anchor lying flat on the ocean floor. When you set the anchor, you let out the appropriate amount of rode and then backed up your boat so that the flukes of the anchor would dig into the bottom. This was what holds, or anchors, your boat. The actual weight of the anchor plays a much smaller role than most people think.

I began to worry I might be boring Molly, but she seemed genuinely interested, even asking me to clarify how the chain kept the anchor flat. I demonstrated it using a tortilla chip and some salsa. I showed her that by keeping the anchor—the chip—flat you could scoop more of the bottom—or salsa. But if you just dipped it in, you would not get much hold, or salsa. She laughed at my analogy but understood the point.

Sitting in the noonday sun and hove to, it began to get quite hot. Molly asked if I minded if she changed into her bathing suit.

"Not at all," I replied.

She went below and peeled off her shirt and pants revealing her fit, tanned, freckled, body in a very sexy orange bikini. Molly obviously took good care of herself. Though she had a nice, shapely, curvy figure, it was also a tight, hard body with hardly an ounce of fat on her. When she came up she handed me her sunscreen and asked me to apply some to her back. She turned her back to me, untied her top and lifted her hair. As I rubbed down her smooth, freckled skin, I felt myself getting excited. Perhaps it had been too long since I'd been with a woman. I worked my way over her shoulders and down her back, under her back strap and down to her panty line. I gave her a playful spank on the cheek when I was done.

"I hope that was as good for you as it was for me?" I playfully asked.

"Not half as good as it could get," as she turned to face me, rubbing my leg.

I took this as my cue and leaned in for a kiss. Molly gratefully accepted, and we kissed long and deep. The ice was broken, and we fed each other's hunger, our mouths open, tongues exploring.

"Well, that was a long time coming," she said smiling as we pulled away.

"Been wanting to do that for a long time," I replied.

I pulled her close, but when she hugged me, I flinched at the pain in my ribs. She pulled back, worried.

"You okay?" she asked, concerned.

"Yeah, I had a little accident this week," I said and pulled up my shirt to show her the bruise that was now an ugly yellow, black, and blue.

"Ooh, what happened?"

"Oh,…stupid, clumsy…fall…tripped." Needless to say I didn't want to tell her about Khakis Sports Jacket or why he had come to see me.

She eyed me up and down, smiling. "You're in pretty good shape, Mike," she said as she placed her palm on my chest. "That fall could have been a lot worse…"

I leaned in for another kiss, pulling her close. To hell with the pain, the pleasure overrode it. I reached up and got a handful of her breast, and her hand slipped down to my crotch. She pulled away and looked around. There were no other boats near us so she undid her top and let it fall. Her breasts were naturally firm and ample, tanned and covered in those magnificent freckles. I caressed them gently as we kissed some more. I wanted to bury my face in them but instead she slid down in front of me on her knees and freed me from my shorts, stroking me. She looked up at me and smiled before taking me in her mouth.

It had been a long time. Not since that fling with the waitress from the Crow's Nest bar. That was over a year ago only lasted about three minutes, and ended up with me too drunk to really enjoy anything. Molly was skillful, and I was feeling blissful. I tried to pull her up to keep my orgasm at bay, telling her I wanted to reciprocate. She told me I'd get my chance and worked me until the pleasure overtook me. It felt like forever, and she wouldn't let up until I was done. I lay back in ecstasy as Molly smiled and took a swig from her Corona. I looked at her with complete pleasure and awe.

"Well, that was fun," she smiled.

I was too taken back to say anything and sat there with a huge shit-eating grin. I reached out to her and she took my hand. I pulled her close in a warm embrace, and she smiled and leaned her head back against my shoulder. We lounged in each other's arms, finishing our beers until we decided to fall off the wind and sail some more.

The rest of the afternoon was a wonderful sail. The wind kept up, moving us along at a steady pace. A pod of dolphins came by, and Molly was ecstatic as they swam alongside us almost close enough to touch. We followed them a ways out in the bay on a beam reach until they vanished in the distance. We then tacked back toward the breakwater, wing on wing, on a run with the wind behind us. Running downwind cut down on the apparent wind, getting hotter in the bright sun. Molly lay back bare-breasted, soaking up the rays as I worked the helm keeping wind in the sails. I still could not believe what had transpired this afternoon and admired her beautiful, tanned, and topless body with a huge grin on my face.

As we got closer to the breakwater, boat traffic picked up and I suggested to Molly that she might want to cover up. She got up, looked around, came over, and gave me a kiss before going below and donning her white shirt over her bare breasts. As we sailed down the main channel, we went over docking procedures and as she took the helm, I furled the jib and started the engine. We motored back to my slip with me at the helm and Molly hugging me from behind.

"Let's go below after we tie her up," she whispered in my ear.

"I do have a nice, comfortable apartment here, you know."

"No, I want to be on the boat," she said.

I smiled brightly and said, "Okay." Molly really was my kind of girl.

But as we pulled into the slip and tied *Stella* up to the dock, Detective Lo and Gomez came walking down the gangway toward us, followed by Andy and Barney, the two uniforms from the night before.

"Uh-oh," I said.

.

CHAPTER 9

Lo was on the dock, waving papers at me. "Michael Millek, we have a warrant to search your property." I took the warrant and looked it over, but it was all legalese to me. It looked official and there was no point arguing it, so I handed it back. Gomez asked Molly if she would step aside so he could ask her a couple of questions. She looked back at me questioningly, but all I could do was shrug my shoulders.

Lo indicated the uniforms to start with *Stella,* so Andy and Barney hopped aboard.

Lo turned back to me. "Mister Millek, do you know a Rudolph Whitley?"

I was too busy watching Molly as Gomez started questioning her and replied off-handedly, "You really know how to fuck up a wet dream, you know that?"

"Mister Millek, do you know Rudolph Whitley?" he repeated.

I finally looked at him, "Rudy? Yeah, of course I do. And I'm sure you know I do. We've been friends since grade school."

"He stole your wife away from you, didn't he?"

"That was a long time ago. He did me a favor."

"So you're still friends?"

"I guess you could say that."

"Then why didn't you tell us last night that he owns a black Charger?"

This got my attention. "What? Rudy owns a black Charger?"

"Don't play stupid, Millek."

I tried to explain to him that Rudy and I only recently started working together and that we hadn't seen each other in almost ten years. I reiterated that I didn't know he owned a black Charger, nor could I imagine him murdering Pays Lee, even if he did owe Rudy a bunch of money. As far as I knew, Rudy didn't even own a gun. And there was certainly more than one black Charger in this town.

Then I saw Molly gasp, throw her hands up to her mouth, and shoot me a look of horror. I grew more concerned when Lo asked me where I'd been since I left the police station last night. I told him I went straight to bed and then out sailing at 10 a.m. this morning. Molly started crying, and I tried to go to her. Lo blocked my way and stuck his fingers in my chest stopping me.

"What the hell is going on?" I demanded.

"Your friend, Rudolph Whitley, is dead."

"What?!" I couldn't believe my ears.

"We found him in his car, out in Temescal Canyon."

"Rudy's dead...?"

"Shot in the head," Lo was watching me to gauge my reaction, which was pretty damned genuine shock. "We need to see the rest of your guns."

"You think I had something to do with it?"

"Procedure," was all he said.

I looked over at Molly who was still upset, and we locked eyes. We were all friends through the years. Me and Rudy, then Sandy and me. Molly and Jimmy. I couldn't believe it.

Andy and Barney then came out from below with my Winchester stainless steel marine pump shotgun and held it up for all to see.

"You didn't mention any shotguns last night," Lo said accusingly.

"You asked me how many handguns I owned, and I told you. Did Rudy get shot with a shotgun?" I asked.

"No."

"Then my shotgun is irrelevant. Come on, you want to see the rest of my guns and search my place? Let's get this over with." I blew past Lo and went to Molly, ignoring Gomez who tried to stop me.

"You okay?" I asked Molly.

"Rudy? I can't believe it," she cried.

"I know." I wrapped my arms around her in a warm embrace, and she buried her face in my shoulder, sobbing.

"Let's go, Millek," barked the inconsiderate Lo.

"You going to be okay getting home?" I asked Molly.

She nodded her head but kept sobbing as I led her up the dock, followed by Santa Monica's finest. When we got to Molly's car, I opened it up for her and packed her and her stuff inside.

Once she was settled, I bent down to her open window. "You sure you're going to be all right?"

Molly sucked in some air and nodded. She started her car, looked up at me and then over at Lo and Gomez, checking to make sure they were out of earshot.

"Mike, you didn't have anything to do with this, did you?" Molly asked.

"Of course not. Please tell me you don't think I did?"

"I just wanted to hear you say it." She pulled me in for a kiss and whispered in my ear, "Call me."

"I will." I held her hand, and we looked deep in each other's eyes.

From behind, Gomez called out, "Ms. Sheehan, we may have some more questions for you later on. Will you be around?"

"I'll be home if you need me", she replied and turned back to me. "Are you going to be okay?"

"Sure. Looks like I've got another long night ahead of me."

With that Gomez stepped up. I blew a kiss to Molly and waved her off. She pulled out, wiping her eyes, and I watched her car drive off.

"Let's go, Millek," said Gomez.

* * *

The cops tore my apartment apart. They found my gun safe with the rest of my handguns as well as my AR-15, my bolt action Enfield, and my lever action .357.

"You've got quite a collection here," said Lo.

"Yeah, well, not as big as some," I replied nonchalantly.

"You prepping for the apocalypse?" asked Gomez half-jokingly.

"No, just the next civil unrest, since the cops seem to go into hiding whenever any big shit happens."

This did not endear me to them any better, and they continued to tear my place apart without any regard for my personal property. When no one was looking directly at me, I eyed my bookshelf, remembering the thumb drive with the incriminating photos and video of Pays Lee and Lauren hidden in my copy of *Moby Dick*. So far, none of the cops went near it. Guess they weren't the literary types either.

Gomez wanted to see my phone, but I told him that was personal and he had no right to look at it. He pulled out the search warrant and pointed out the fact that he did have the right to see my call records and emails. Reluctantly, I unlocked it and handed it over.

I gave up trying to help them and sat back on the sofa while Gomez went through my calls and text messages. I started thinking of Rudy and tried to wrap my head around the fact that he was dead. I couldn't believe that it was Rudy who took a shot at me and gave chase in the Charger. No way that was him. Rudy might have a street-smart felonious streak in him, but he wasn't a killer any more than I was.

A thought occurred to me. "Hey, has anyone called Rudy's family?".

"Notified his ex-wife, your ex-wife, to identify the body. She thinks you had something to do with it," said Lo.

"Figures. That why you're tearing my place apart? I mean,

what are you looking for? If you tell me, maybe I can help you," I said.

"We're looking for the money, amongst other things," said Gomez.

"What money?" I said playing it as dumb as I could.

"Pays Lee's money, hotshot," piped Lo.

"And why would you think I have Pays Lee's money?" I asked.

Gomez chimed in, "We know Pays left Vegas with a large amount of cash, and apparently"—he came to the text from Pays and showed me the picture of him holding the red bag full of cash—"so did you."

I was numb by then. I knew they'd throw that photo at me as soon as they found it. But I also knew they'd probably gone through Pays Lee's phone and seen that he'd sent it to me, so I was ready.

"I told you he owed me money, so I wasn't going to pick him up. Until he sent me that picture," I explained. "I thought I would finally get paid."

Gomez checked the call logs and saw that I called Rudy shortly thereafter.

"Looks like you were giving your friend the heads-up. That how he knew when and where Pays was coming in?" asked Gomez.

"No, Rudy didn't pick up. I left a message saying I got a call from Pays and for him to call me back so I could fill him in. But he never called back."

Gomez looked at me doubtfully as if he were digesting what I told him.

"If you have Rudy's phone you can probably hear my message, assuming he didn't delete it," I said. I figured they probably had already.

"Oh, we will," he said, covering his tracks, still not sure what to make of this.

I decide to change the subject and asked if I could take a

shower. Being out on the water left me salty and sticky. I wanted to clean up. Both Gomez and Lo were hesitant. I pointed out there was no window in the bathroom so there was no way I could "escape," and I promised not to drown myself. Reluctantly they let me go as long as I didn't lock the door. As I stripped down to shower, I started wondering about Rudy's family back east. His pop passed away a while back, but I didn't know if his mom was still alive. He had a younger sister who I hadn't seen in ages. Last I heard she was married and living somewhere in Florida. I wondered if she knew, or if I was the one who was going to have to break it to her.

The more I thought about Rudy, the more I realized how much he meant to me and how much I owed him. And how much I loved him. If it weren't for him, I never would have learned to sail, never would have moved to California, and never would have had the life I lived. Rudy was the brother I never had. I was sorry that Sandy came between us and that we were out of touch for so long. By time I got out of the shower and was drying off, I decided it was my duty to call Rudy's family and was hoping the police would give me back my phone to do so. Instead, Lo banged on the door.

"Come on, Millek. Get some clothes on. We're taking you to the station."

I opened the door to face Lo wearing a towel. "What for?" I asked.

"You're under arrest as an accessory to the murder of Pays Lee," he smirked.

"Are you fucking serious?" I looked past Lo to Gomez.

Gomez nodded toward the closet. "Get dressed."

My dream day sailing with Molly was now beginning to turn into a nightmare.

CHAPTER 10

I was put into the same interrogation room at the Santa Monica Police Department for take two. Left alone again for forty-five minutes to presumably sweat it out. Instead of making me sweat, all it did was piss me off. I knew this was a bullshit rap. My only worry was that some security camera at the airport revealed something. But I put that out of my mind, figuring they would have found that earlier, put the screws to me, and booked me sooner. They had nothing to prove I had anything to do with Pays Lee's or Rudy's murders. Even if they knew I had the money—which I knew they didn't—they could not connect me with the killing. They didn't find the thumb drive either. As we were leaving, I saw *Moby Dick* sitting on my bookshelf right where I left it. Since I was dog-tired after just a couple of hours of sleep the night before plus all day out in the sun with Molly on the boat, it wasn't too hard to put my head on the table and take a snooze.

Gomez and Lo finally came in and slammed a legal pad down on the table, waking me up. They began right away.

"So Mike, you going to make some points with the judge and come clean?" asked Gomez.

"You're looking at a triple homicide. That's the needle, boy," Lo threw in.

"Look, I know you guys didn't find a damn thing at my place to link me to any of this. You're blowing smoke," I told them as I rubbed the sleep from my eyes.

Gomez spelled it out, "We know you and Rudy were planning to take down Pays Lee. You tipped him off to do the dirty work. You arrived late to try and cement your alibi. You hook up with Rudy at your rendezvous point, shoot him in the head, and stick him in the trunk while you grab the money and run."

"Wait a second," I said, leaning forward on the edge of my seat. "You found Rudy in the trunk?"

"Don't play dumb, asshole," said Lo.

"You're the only asshole here, Charlie Chan," I shot back, not meaning to get as carried away as did.

Lo was quick and kicked the chair out from under me, landing me on the floor. He was coming for me while I was down, but Gomez grabbed him and pulled him away. I saw Gomez glance at the two-way mirror in the room. Somebody important must have been watching, maybe their captain or the assistant D.A. assigned to the case.

"That's it, I want my lawyer." I got back into my chair, pulled it up to the table, and folded my hands together like a well-behaved schoolboy.

They continued to try and get me to talk, but I replied to all their questions with, "Lawyer." After another ten minutes of this, they left the room.

I had no idea who I'd call. Who was I kidding? I had no lawyer. A public defender? There was a tenant at the Tiki Marina Apartments I casually knew who was a lawyer. Or that blow-hard ambulance-chaser attorney who fancies himself an actor and who seems to get cast as an extra on every film I've worked on for the past five years. No, I needed someone with connections. Then it dawned on me—Jonathan Pichter. He not only had connections and clout, he might actually be involved in this. It got me thinking. He had motive. Was seeing those images of Pays and Lauren enough for him to have Pays Lee killed? Could the killer have been Khakis Sport Jacket? If Pichter were somehow involved, how did Rudy fit into the picture, and why was he killed? I was still trying to wrap my head around it all when Gomez and Lo re-entered the room and held the door open.

"Okay, let's go," Gomez said indicating the door. Both he and Lo looked like they got chewed out by whoever was behind that mirror.

"Where we going?"

"To call your lawyer," Gomez said. He and Lo led me down the corridor to the bullpen where his desk was. He sat me down, and Lo shoved a desk phone in front of me. Lo was obviously pissed off, and I got some pleasure from this.

"I need my phone," I said.

"Forget it. It's evidence," said Lo.

"His number's on my phone."

Gomez looked to Lo, who stormed off.

It was tensely quiet between me and Gomez for the ten minutes Lo was gone. I tried to think how I was going to make the most powerful lawyer in Hollywood take my call at 10:00 p.m. on a Sunday night. He was my one ace in the hole, and I had to play it. When Lo came back, he placed the cellphone in front of me and watched as I went through my phone pictures until I found the photo I'd taken of Jonathan Pichter's business card.

"Don't be deleting anything," he said. "That's evidence."

I gave him a dirty look and dialed the number on the desk phone.

"How about some privacy?" I said.

Lo fumed as he and Gomez retreated to the far corner of the room to give me some space.

"Pichter, Loam, and Stein," said a pleasant female voice.

"Hello, I need to speak with Mr. Pichter, please."

"I'm sorry but Mr. Pichter won't be in the office until tomorrow. Can I take a message?"

Of course he wasn't in the office.

"This is kind of an emergency. It's regarding his daughter. Is there a way you can page him, or call him at home," I pleaded.

"I'm sorry, this is the answering service. We're not authorized to call or page Mr. Pichter on the weekends."

I suddenly remembered something. "Of course not. Thank you," I said and quickly hung up.

I looked at my phone again and went through the pictures as Gomez and Lo approached. "I need to call him at another number," I said, stopping them. They went back to the corner, watching me.

I scanned the photos and finally found the one I was looking for—the photo I had taken of Javier's phone. It was the number Lauren had called when she left my boat that morning. I was betting it was Pichter's cell or home number. Hoping I was right, and that he would pick up, I dialed the number.

"Who is this?" was all he said.

"Hello, my name is Mike Millek. I'm under arrest at the Santa Monica Police station for the murder of Pays Lee."

"I'm sorry, I can't help you," said Pichter.

I had to get his attention before he hung up. I cupped the phone and turned my back to Gomez and Lo.

"I think you can, sir. I believe the police will be very interested in seeing some photos and a video I have in my possession of the late Mister Pays Lee and a young woman." I let that sink in before I added, "I believe her name is Lauren."

There was a deafening silence on the other end. I gave it a few moments and said, "Hello?" I worried he might have hung up.

"Have they seen the photos?"

"No, sir," I said trying to assure him, then added, "No one has."

"Someone will be there within the hour."

I tried to thank him, but he had already hung up. I said thank you into the phone anyway for the benefit of Gomez and Lo.

I was put in a holding cell with a homeless guy who smelled like he'd either been pissing his pants for the last month or getting pissed on for the last month. I tried to keep my distance upwind of him as he slept stretched out on the bench.

I didn't really think anyone would show within the hour but

was surprised when Gomez came to get me after seventy-five minutes. Pichter was taking this seriously. Maybe he *was* involved, and I threw a monkey wrench into his plan. Gomez took me back to the interrogation room. Sitting there was a straight-laced African-American man, sharply dressed in a conservative Brooks Brothers suit and a starched French blue shirt complete with a yellow print bow tie. He looked like he just walked out of the University Club and rose from his chair to shake my hand as I approached.

"Mister Millek, my name is Morris Bigsby. Jonathan Pichter sent me."

He handed me his card. It stated his name and that he was a Criminal Defense Attorney.

"I appreciate you coming on such short notice, and on a Sunday evening, Mister Bigsby," I said.

"Not a problem." Bigsby looked over my shoulder and waited until Gomez left the room.

"I understand you have something that belongs to Mister Pichter," he continued.

"Well, actually, it doesn't belong to Mister Pichter. But what we need to discuss is getting me out of here." I tried to steer the conversation to my current situation.

"The paperwork is being processed as we speak. We'll be leaving shortly," he said calmly with confidence. These guys didn't fool around.

"You're bailing me out?" I asked.

"The district attorney has dropped the charges. They don't have any real reason to hold you. The evidence is purely circumstantial. They were simply trying to intimidate you to see if they could make a case."

"I see. Thank you."

"Mister Pichter would like to speak with you upon your release," Bigsby said as he rose. "There will be a car outside, waiting for you."

"For me? Look, I've had a long day…" I started.

"You can always spend the night here," Bigsby said, indicating I did not have a choice in the matter. He paused at the door to make sure I understood.

"I'll be there," I responded.

"A wise decision, Mister Millek. Good evening." With that, he was out the door.

Five minutes later, Gomez came in with my phone, wallet, my folding knife, my laptop computer, and the rest of my personal belongings. He escorted me out, past a pissed-off Lo who gave me the evil eye. Gomez led me to down the stairs toward a back door to the building.

"I don't know how you did it, Millek, but I *will* get to the bottom of this," he said.

"It was easy. You got the wrong guy. And you knew it. You want to get to the bottom of it, go find the real killer," I told him, no longer feeling the need to be cordial.

Gomez stopped at the door, blocking it, and looked at me with contempt. "I know you know more than you're letting on, Millek."

"I have no reason to lie," I lied. "I already told you everything I know, Detective."

He continued to eye me but I matched his stare, not giving in or giving anything away. We stared at each other for a few seconds before he opened the door. "Stay out of trouble," he said as he looked off at the black Mercedes-Maybach that sat idling nearby. I recognized it as the car that picked up Lauren from the Tiki Marina Apartments surveillance video.

The windows were blacked out and as I approached, the driver stepped out. My ribs suddenly ached when I saw it was Khakis Sport Jacket, dressed more casually tonight in an all-black warm-up suit. I stopped in my tracks until he smiled, opened the back door and nodded toward it. I approached and saw someone in there. Still eying Khakis Sport Jacket, I cautiously got in.

"So you're Millek," came the voice seated beside me. It was a well-kept, slight, tanned, and silver-haired older gentleman.

"And you must be Jonathan Pichter," I responded.

I would have guessed he was close to seventy but based on appearance looking closer to sixty. Money can do that to people. Make them appear younger. Money and good living, Pichter obviously had both. He was dressed crisp and fresh in casual, tasteful slacks, shirt, and sport jacket, like he was going to dinner at the country club. Not what you would imagine for someone being dragged from his home close to midnight on a Sunday night. He eyed me with mixture of curiosity and contempt. Khakis Sport Jacket eyed me in the rearview until he threw the car in gear and drove off.

"You mentioned you have something that belongs to my daughter," said Pichter.

"Not really," I said.

Both Pichter and Khakis Sport Jacket gave me a quick look.

"But on the phone you said…"

"I was bluffing," I told them. "Yes, I've seen the pictures because your daughter left her phone in my car, and I went through it to find out how I could return it. That was until you sent Oddjob here to rough me up," I said indicating his driver.

"Rough you up?" He and Khakis Sport Jacket eyed each other in the rearview before turning his attention back to me. "Well, then I owe you an apology, Mister Millek. Carl is usually very well-mannered."

"Could have fooled me." Carl and I traded looks in the rearview.

"He's also very protective of my family. As am I, naturally. Which is why I would like to get any copies of those pictures you might have."

"Like I said, I was bluffing. I don't have any."

I was happy to see we were heading south on Nielsen Way back toward the marina, and I figured I might as well tell him the whole story. Well, most of the story. I explained how Pays Lee left Lauren with me with instructions to drop her off at Butch's, what happened afterwards, and how I was about to drop her phone off at his office when Carl decided to play soccer on my ribs.

He studied me for a few minutes before asking, "And what about Mister Lee's death? Did you have something to do with that?" he asked.

"I was about to ask you the same thing," I told him.

"Me? I am not a murderer."

"And neither am I. But what about Carl? You said he's very protective of your family."

I got another look from Carl in the rearview.

"Judging from those pictures, you would certainly have more motive than me," I said. "I assume that's why you bailed me out."

"I didn't bail you out, Mister Millek. The charges were dropped, for now—lack of evidence. Mister Lee was carrying a large amount of cash when he left Las Vegas. Upwards of eight hundred thousand. And now that money is gone," he said eyeing me.

"I wouldn't know anything about that," I said, trying hard not to show my surprise at how he knew about the money and how much. Eight hundred grand! I now realized just how hot the potato I was holding was.

"That's quite a motive for murder."

"I imagine it would be. But you knew he had that money. I didn't," I said.

"So you say."

"How would I know? You think that's something Pays Lee would share with me? Besides, a good friend of mine was killed last night as well."

"Omar?"

"No, not Omar."

"Ah, yes, the other victim. In the car. My condolences. Perhaps *he* had something to do with Mister Lee's murder? That's what the police believe."

"I don't think so," I told him.

"It is my understanding that your friend was owed a large sum of money by Mister Lee."

"Not enough worth killing for. Or getting killed for." I wondered where he got his information. He was obviously privy to the police investigation or someone tipped him off about Rudy.

Pichter spoke soft and slowly, "You'd be surprised what people would do for that kind of money. And the reality is, the money is missing and your friend is dead. It would be reasonable to believe he probably found out Mister Lee was holding a large amount of money and thought he could cash in. But perhaps someone else knew and was partnered with your friend. Someone who decided they didn't want to split it." When he finished speaking, he turned and looked at me. "It makes perfect sense for the police to suspect you, no?"

"Assuming my friend, his name was Rudy, by the way..."

"Yes, Rudolph, I know," said Pichter.

"Assuming *Rudy* killed Pays Lee, there's no way I would have had the time to run up to Temescal Canyon, murder him, stash the money, and be back on Lincoln where I called it in to the police," I explained. "After that I was with the police the rest of the night."

"Which is most likely why you're not in jail now."

"Gee, and I thought you had something to do with that. I'm sorry I bothered you," I said.

"You should be," he said and then got serious. "I want those pictures and the video, Mister Millek. I think I've held up my part of this bargain."

"Like I said, I was bluffing." I offered him my laptop. "Here, you can check my computer if you like. I'm sure the police have, and I guarantee you there are no pictures or videos of your daughter. And I didn't mention a thing about them to the police. You have my word."

Pichter looked from me to my laptop and back at me with piercing eyes as we pulled up to Tiki Marina. I gave him the best innocent face I could muster.

"I'm sorry about what happened to your daughter, sir. The truth is, those pictures deeply disturbed me. And to be quite honest, I think Pays Lee probably got what he deserved. Your daughter seems like a sweet girl who got caught up in something she probably thought was exciting and got taken advantage of. I would not want to do anything to hurt her any further than she's already been hurt," I said honestly.

Pichter was still staring at me, sizing me up, but then he nodded. "I appreciate that, Mister Millek."

"But I will find out who killed my friend." I looked from Pichter to Carl, eyeing me in the rearview.

"And how do you plan to do that?"

"Any way I can."

"Then I wish you all the best," as he held out his hand.

I shook his hand. "Thank you for expediting my release."

"You owe me for that, Mister Millek."

"Why don't we call it even for me keeping certain information from the police." I nodded toward Carl who was already out of the car and opening my door, before adding, "And for my cracked ribs."

Pichter smiled, "Very well, Mister Millek."

As I got out, my eyes met Carl's. They were cold and heartless. I felt like he could, and would kill me, with little more thought than stomping on a cockroach. Could he be Pays Lee's killer? And Rudy's? I wasn't sure, but I wouldn't put it past him.

"Goodnight...Carl," I said more to cover my fear than show any bravado.

He closed the rear door of the Maybach and got back behind the wheel, eyes on me the whole time. His look sent a shiver down my spine just like that ice-cold drop from the elevated IRT train in The Bronx so long ago.

CHAPTER 11

I checked *Moby Dick* the moment I got home and was relieved to see the thumb drive was still there. My apartment was a mess. The police had ransacked the place, but I was too dog-tired to deal with any of it. I poured myself a couple of fingers of Patrón from the freezer, sat down on the couch, and tried to wrap my head around what had happened in the last forty-eight hours. I had to be at work in a couple of hours and didn't know whether I should try to sleep or make a pot of coffee and straighten up a bit. I thought should call Chris DeLuca and give him a heads-up about Rudy and all that was happening. I also wanted to reach out to Rudy's sister, but I hadn't spoke to her in years. I wasn't even sure I'd be able to track her down.

A big part of me wanted to go check out the money. Eight hundred grand! Could that really be true? It didn't seem like there could be *that* much in the bag, but what did I know.

My head was aching, so I got up and went out onto the terrace to get some air. I took a couple of deep breaths and immediately felt better. The night was cool, damp, and salty. The breakwater foghorn blew in the distance. Halyards rattled against their masts and rang out in the light breeze. I could see *Stella* out there amongst all the other boats on the dock finger. Sailing with Molly, and what transpired between us, felt like years ago. I wanted to call her but it was way too late. Then I remembered my phone. It was off, and when I turned it on, I was happy to see there was a text from her.

"Everything OK?" she had written about two hours ago.

"OK now. Finally back home," I texted back figuring she'd see it when she woke up.

Seconds later the phone rang. It was Molly. I hit the connect button and said, "What are you doing up?"

"I couldn't sleep. Are you okay?" she asked.

I told her I was and filled her in on the search and getting taken in and questioned again. I pretty much told her everything I knew about Rudy, the Pays Lee murders, and how I was a suspect. I still left out the part about the money, plus now Pichter, Carl, Bigsby, et al.

"I was worried about you. Those detectives seemed like they meant business."

"They were just being assholes. But under the circumstances, I guess it was kind of understandable," I said, thinking of my conversation with Pichter.

"What's going to happen with Rudy?"

"I'm guessing they'll probably do an autopsy before they release his body. Then I don't know. Guess I'll have to try and get in touch with Sandy or his family to see what they want, what his wishes were, if he had any," I thought out loud.

"I still can't believe it," she said exasperated.

"I know. Neither can I."

"You guys were pretty close."

"Yeah. Since we were kids," I said.

There was an awkward, sad silence between us until, "Hey, thanks for the sailing. I had a really good time," she said.

"Me too. I'm sorry it ended the way it did."

"Mike, if there's anything I can do…?" she offered.

Yeah, there's plenty you could do, I thought to myself, remembering our afternoon together. And those freckles.

But instead I said, "Thanks, I appreciate it. I'll let you know if there is."

I was still staring out over the marina when I noticed

something. Below me in the boaters' parking lot, someone was sitting in a dark-colored Mustang, directly across from my apartment. I could barely see it and had to strain my eyes to see. All I could make out was the outline of a figure behind the wheel. He had to be watching me, since I was no more than forty feet away from him.

"Mike...?" Molly broke the silence.

"Yeah?"

"Are you going to be okay?" she asked.

"Me? Yeah, sure. What about you? You okay?"

"I'm still trying to absorb it all, I guess."

"I know. It's...crazy."

The person in the Mustang wasn't moving, but I knew he was watching me. I thought of heading out there under the guise of checking on *Stella*, to see if I could get a better look. But then I thought better of it. I didn't want any kind of confrontation, especially unarmed. Could it be someone involved in the murder? Someone looking for the money? Someone involved with Pichter? Then I realized it was probably a police tail. Of course they'd be watching me.

"I guess I should let you go. You must be dead t...I mean, tired," said Molly.

"I know what you meant. Yeah, I guess I am. I was trying to decide whether to try and sleep for a couple of hours or just stay up."

I went back inside, locked the sliding glass door, and drew the curtains.

"We should both probably try and get some sleep," she said.

"You're probably right. I guess I'll see you in a couple of hours."

"You should call off, Mike. No one would blame you under the circumstances."

"I know, but I should at least show up and explain things. Fill Chris in about Rudy and all. Hopefully he'll cut me loose."

"I'm sure he will. Goodnight, Mike."

"Goodnight, Molly. Thanks for calling."

I hung up and went to the bedroom window to see if I could get a better look at the man in the Mustang. He was still there, but all I could see was his unmoving silhouette. Maybe I was seeing things, my eyes playing tricks on me. I rubbed them as I fell back on the bed. I was out before my head hit the pillow.

My phone alarm woke me from a deep sleep, in a cold sweat. I'd been having a weird dream involving a naked Lauren, laughing as she squatted over Pays Lee's blown-open head and peeing on his mushed brains. It creeped me out, and it took me a moment to gather my bearings. I remembered the Mustang and peeked out the window. Gone. Maybe my eyes had been playing tricks on me?

I stumbled into the bathroom for a wake-up shower.

As I walked to the Suburban in the garage, I felt as I was being watched, even though I scoured the area and saw no one. The Mustang was nowhere in sight. It was still dark out as I headed over to the studio, and I continued scanning my mirrors to see if I was being followed. When I arrived at the studio, Chris DeLuca was in the process of moving all our equipment off the lot and to a shooting location downtown L.A. Directing truck traffic, Chris was barking into his walkie talkie to his drivers, leading the movie caravan out the studio gates. He looked surprised to see me.

"Mike, what are you doing here?" he said.

"I guess you heard." I asked.

"Yeah, what the hell...?"

I shrugged, "I don't know. It's all so...fucked."

"Hey, I'm sorry. I know you and Rudy were real close. At least you were...I mean, back when."

"We were close, Chris," I said. "It's been years but this show brought us back together. You brought us back together. He was the best friend I ever had."

Chris asked me about what went down with the police, and I knew he was wondering if I had anything to do with Rudy's death. I filled him in as best I could and let him know that they had nothing on me and that's why they cut me loose. He looked at me a bit more trustingly and told me I should head home.

"I got you covered," he said. "Do what you gotta do and call me in a couple of days. I know it must be rough."

"I appreciate that, Chris. I should call his family and..."

"Sandy?" he asked.

"I guess." I said not looking forward to that. "You know she told the cops I probably had something to do with it?"

"Ex-wives, gotta love 'em," he smirked.

"Yeah, right," I said. "Well, thanks. I'll keep you in the loop."

We shook hands before I got back in the Suburban and headed back to the marina. I called Molly from the car and filled her in about Chris giving me a couple of days off. She was happy to hear it and offered to come by after the day's wrap. I told her that would be great.

I got back to my place and looked long and hard at my phone screen with Sandy's phone number staring back at me before I had the nerve to hit the call button. She picked up after five rings.

"Why aren't you in jail?" was how she answered.

"Because the police couldn't prove I had anything to do with it, no thanks to you," I said.

"Hey! They asked me if Rudy had any enemies, and you were the only one I could think of," she said.

"What about yourself?" I asked.

"I didn't have anything against him."

"Of course not. You just fucked around on him, like you did with me."

"It's not like that," she said.

"That's exactly what you told me when you fucked around behind *my* back."

"This was different," she retorted.

"Right. I guess this time it must have been love."

"Fuck you!" she fired back.

"There's the Sandy I know and love," and I laughed.

"You're an asshole. Why are you even calling me?" she asked.

"I wanna know if you've been in touch with Rudy's family."

"Why would I? We split up over a year ago."

"Thought you might have some decency left in you."

"They hate me."

"Can you blame them?"

"Fuck off, Michael."

"So, I guess it's up to me to break the news. You by chance have any phone numbers?"

Sandy informed me that Rudy's mother had passed away a few years back. The only number she had was for his younger sister, Jennifer, who was divorced and living in Florida. Jenny was a couple of years younger than us but just as wild back when we spent summers in Maine. She was sort of a cute tomboy back then, and whenever Rudy and I scored some beers she wasn't far behind bumming from us. I remember she blossomed into a fine-looking fox who could hold her own with any guy she went out with. As good looking as she was, she was one tough chick, and I would have been more scared of her than her older brother if I were her boyfriend. I hadn't seen her since before I moved to California. Rudy used to mumble something about her loser husband, and I felt it was because of him she and Rudy fell out of touch. According to Sandy, they reestablished contact after Jenny got divorced. She had a couple of kids and had gone through rehab. Apparently she'd gotten hooked on crystal meth and alcohol, and it was Rudy who paid for her treatment and was sending her money every month. Sandy said she'd cleaned herself up, "but you know addicts. Who knows what she was up to." Sandy always had a way of putting everyone else down. There was no love lost between us, and I was happy to end my call with her.

I dialed Jenny's number as soon as I got off the phone with Sandy.

"Hello?" she answered in her hoarse, husky voice after several rings.

"Hi, is this Jenny?"

"Who wants to know?"

"It's Mike. Mike Millek, from The Bronx."

It took her a few moments for that to sink in before, "Holy shit!" she exclaimed happily.

It was good to hear her voice, which made it even harder to break the news of her brother's death. She took it better than I thought she would or maybe she just put on a brave front. I filled her in on the details regarding what little I knew about the investigation, the coroner's contact information, and offered to help out in any way I could. She was appreciative and told me she'd been out to see Rudy a few times in the last couple of years since she had gotten divorced. She reminisced how Rudy had taken her and her two teenage kids to Magic Mountain and Universal Studios. We caught up a bit and touched a little on old times. She seemed on the straight and narrow now, a couple of times she even referenced Jesus, which made me think she had found religion as part of her rehab. I sensed that the more she reminisced, the more it was starting to hit her that Rudy was gone. By time we ended our call, she was crying. I promised to help out in any way I could and gave her my number. She thanked me before we hung up.

I didn't know what her plans would be for Rudy's body, but I knew that the Pays Lee money would help out in some way. This prompted me to think again about the cash. I decided I'd better go check on it. Make sure it was still there. Make sure this wasn't all part of some crazy dream. Or the nightmare it seemed to come from.

CHAPTER 12

I was planning on walking over to C Basin to Ari Goldman's *Above the Line* when I saw the Mustang parked out front of the building. I couldn't tell if anyone was in it. So instead of walking, I went downstairs into the garage to get the Suburban. I drove out and got about halfway down Tonga Way when in my rearview I saw the Mustang pull out of the Tiki parking lot. As I drove around the marina, I kept my eyes on him. I made a couple of unnecessary turns to confirm that the Mustang was indeed following me. It was, and the driver wasn't a very good tail if he was trying to be slick about it. I still didn't know who it was—Gomez or Lo? One of their lackeys from the Santa Monica P.D.? And if it wasn't them, who was it?

I pulled down Mindanao Way to H Basin on the opposite side of the marina where a grip I knew, Peter Darcy, lived on his Catalina 36. I'd looked after his boat on many occasions when he was out of town working on location. My plan was to park in his marina's lot, borrow his inflatable dinghy, and head over to *Above the Line* via the water. In the meantime, I dug out the little point-and-shoot camera that I kept in the glove compartment that shoots time-lapse video. I thought if I could set it up inconspicuously inside the Suburban maybe I could get a shot of my shadow if he came over to check out my vehicle.

After setting up my camera on the armrest of the passenger door, I got out and approached Peter's slip gate. I punched in the security code and walked down the gangway. I did my best not to look back to see if the Mustang was there so I wouldn't give away that I knew I was being followed. When I got to Peter's boat, I saw the companionway was open, so I called out.

"Ahoy, Peter, you in there?"

Peter's head popped up, and he smiled when he saw me.

"Hey, Mike! What's going on?"

We exchanged pleasantries, and Peter wiped his greasy hands on a rag before we shook hands. He explained he had replaced his old Atomic Four engine with a newer Yanmar diesel he'd got a deal on. He'd just had it installed, but there was some air in his fuel line and was trying to bleed it. I hopped in and gave it a look. Closing the bleed screw, I told him to give it a try. As Peter tried the starter, I took a quick look back at the parking lot. Sure enough, the Mustang was there. Peter's engine started right up and he was ecstatic, thanking me for the help. We chatted a bit while the engine idled, making small talk, and I found out Peter had done some pre-rigging at Sony for the Rossi picture. He had a regular gig on a sitcom that was shooting up in the valley at Warner's but was off today.

"Listen, I was wondering if I could ask a favor?" I said.

"Sure. As long as it doesn't cost me anything," he joked. "This engine set me back."

"Not at all. Was wondering if I could borrow your dinghy for about half an hour." I didn't want to arouse any suspicion as to why I needed the dinghy so I made up a quick little story. "I got a client's boat over in C basin I have to check on and my security code's not working on his dock gate."

"Sure, go ahead," he nodded toward the Zodiac inflatable tied up at his stern. "Your client not pay his slip fees?" he asked.

When boaters are late with their slip fees, some marinas lock their security gate codes so they can't get access to their boat.

"Could be. I don't know. He's been out of town for a while," I said.

"Well, make sure you get paid."

"I always do," I replied. "One way or another," I added under my breath.

I went over to the dinghy, untied the dock lines, hopped in, and shoved off. Two seconds later, I started the little putt-putt outboard with the pull cord, glancing back to see the Mustang's door open. I smiled to myself as I motored across the main channel toward C Basin. It felt good to be out on the water. It was still pretty early, and there weren't many boats out in the channel yet. The fresh salt air revived me after not getting much sleep the last couple of nights. I took several deep breaths relishing the moment as I made my way across the main channel.

Above the Line was about halfway down C basin on the far side of the channel, so there was no way anyone could have seen where I was going from Peter's marina. Even if Mustang Man had binoculars, there were several apartment buildings blocking his view. I arrived and tied up at the end tie of the finger dock, so if someone was on the landside of the dock, they wouldn't be able to see the dinghy. I hustled over to *Above the Line* and hopped aboard before any prying eyes could notice. As I opened the cabin, I stopped in my tracks—I heard voices.

"Who's there?!" It was Ari Goldman, with his thick Israeli accent. I froze.

"It's me, Ari. Mike Millek."

Ari came running up from the master suite to greet me. He was dressed in only a towel wrapped around his big belly. Ari was probably in his late sixties and the salt and pepper hair on his chest grew up to his shoulders and around to his back. The thick gold chain and Star of David around his neck contrasted with his tanned body.

"Oh, it's you."

"I'm sorry, Ari, I didn't know you were back in town," I said.

"I'm not! And if anyone asks, you didn't see me," he smiled slyly.

"Of course." I was trying to figure out as to why Ari was back so unannounced, why the secrecy, and how I was going to get to the money. Then I got the answer.

"Who is it, Ari?" It was a woman's voice.

She came out, wrapping herself in a silk kimono. She was gorgeous—a chestnut brunette with blond streaks and striking ice-blue eyes. She had an incredibly sexy body, curvy, voluptuous, and perfectly proportioned. And she was at least forty years younger than Ari. He said something to her in Hebrew before he introduced me.

"Michael, this is Yael Idelson, the top supermodel in all of Tel Aviv."

"Pleasure to meet you" I said for lack of anything else to say.

"Hello." She approached, looked at me mischievously concupiscent, and offered her hand. We shook. Her hand was soft and moist.

"She's going to be a big star here in Hollywood," Ari gushed.

This made Yael smile and sidle up next to him, putting her arm around him.

"I'm sure," I said.

"I am going to put her in a series of action pictures," Ari said more to her than to me, and she ate up his bullshit, hook, line, and sinker. "She's very athletic." He smiled at her.

"That's wonderful! I'm so sorry to interrupt. I came by to check on the automatic bilge pump. It's been acting up," I lied.

Ari tore himself away from her, came over to me, and led me out the stern door.

"Don't worry about the bilge pump, right now. Listen…" he said, making sure Yael was out of earshot. "She's going to be staying here, so I won't need you checking on the boat for a while. And I don't want you saying anything to anyone."

I nodded, "Of course."

Knowing Ari was married, it made perfect sense keeping her here. But still thinking of the money, I had to try and grab an opening.

"But Ari, I do need to finish some work I started. Otherwise, the boat, she could sink."

"What? No! The boat is not sinking. Don't worry."

"I'll come by when there's no one here. Just let me know, and I'll get everything all fixed up for you."

"Good, good. But for now, we need a little privacy," he winked. "You understand, right."

"Absolutely."

He looked back inside the salon as Yael lounged, leg over the arm of the settee she was sitting on, waiting for him. The clinging silk kimono, open to her waist left little to the imagination. He elbowed me conspiratorially, "She's hot, no?"

"Very," I smiled.

"And she loves to fuck. So, please, leave us."

There was no way I was going to get to the money, and I couldn't help picturing them fucking right above it on the bed in the master stateroom.

"Of course, but please let me know. I don't want the boat sinking under you."

"The boat will not sink."

"All I need is a half an hour or so…"

"Okay, okay. I will call you," and he hustled me off the stern.

I got back in the dinghy and started it up, trying to figure out my next move. This was a predicament. Ari Goldman had been out of the country for like eleven months and *now* he shows up? When I just happened to have eight hundred thousand dollars in cold hard cash stashed under the bed that he's banging his hot Israeli mistress on? It might be days before he leaves his boat with that hottie. I know it would be if I were in his shoes. My only hope was that they would go out to eat or she would want him to show her the town. But what if they decided to change the sheets and looked in the storage locker under the mattress? I had to come up with a way to get them off that boat for a short time. I also had to figure out where to stash the money once I was able to grab it.

I putt-putted down the basin and turned toward B Basin to cruise by *Stella* and Tiki Marina. I don't know why, but I wanted to make sure nothing was amiss. Sometimes you can see things clearer from the water than you can being right there. I also wanted to confuse Mustang Man in case he was watching for my return, as I was almost sure he was.

Nothing seemed out of the ordinary at Tiki Marina, but seeing *Stella* from the water gave me an idea. I started to formulate a plan about to where to hide the money once I was able to get it. Satisfied, I turned the dinghy around and headed back across the main channel to H Basin and Peter's boat. The whole way back, all I did was try to figure out a way to get Ari and his girlfriend off his boat for a while so I could grab the money. The first thing I had to do was get Mustang Man off my back, and I was hoping my camera might shed some light on that problem. Who could this mystery man be? The more I thought about it, the more I was hoping it was a cop. If he wasn't, then there was a good chance he was the killer. He'd be the only one who knew I had the money, and that was the reason he was following me.

I pulled up to Peter's slip, killed the putt-putt, and secured the dinghy to Peter's dock. He popped out of his companionway to greet me, his engine still running.

"She's running great," Peter said.

"Huh? Oh yeah...sounds like it," I agreed.

"Thanks for helping me bleed that fuel line. I was at it for like an hour before you showed up," he said.

"No problem," I said, neglecting to inform him that his new used engine actually had a self-bleeding fuel line feature and that he didn't need to do it manually. "Thanks for letting me borrow your dinghy."

"You get everything done?" he asked.

"Not really, I'm going to have to go back with my tools." Bringing my big canvas tool bag would be a good way to smuggle the money off *Above the Line*.

"Well, if you need the dinghy again, come on by," he offered as I hoped he would, without asking what was wrong with my inflatable.

"Thanks."

"If I'm not here, help yourself."

"Sweet. Thanks, I appreciate it," I said as I said goodbye and headed back to the parking lot.

I went for my Suburban, and I noticed the Mustang wasn't where I last saw it. But after a look around, I noticed it was parked further down the lot near the exit, like the driver was trying hide or be inconspicuous. A little late for that, I thought to myself. Getting in, the first thing I did was check the camera.

I watched the time-lapse video, not seeing much movement except for light changing as clouds passed in front of the sun. Then—bingo. I paused the video and rewound until I came to one clear still frame of Mustang Man cupping his face and peering into the Suburban. He was a swarthy, dark haired, wiry, muscle-bound guy in a wife beater and gold chain, with a mustache and goatee. I didn't recognize him and had already ruled him out as being with the police based on the way he was dressed and how bad and obvious a tail he was. Either way, I wanted to get him off my ass. I decided to up the ante and test my theory as I checked him out in my rear-view mirror. He was parked close to the street, boxed in, with a small convertible roadster parked in front of him so I whipped a U-turn. I was betting that if he were the killer, he wouldn't try to kill me in broad daylight in a fairly busy marina. I drove up right behind him stopping perpendicular to him, blocking him in, and took a picture of his license plate. I waited there and looked at the photo to make sure I could read the plate number clearly. The Mustang started up and the back-up lights came on. I held my ground until he beeped his horn. I wanted to see him come out so I could take another picture of him, but he just kept beeping the horn. I got an idea. I threw the Suburban in park, jumped out with my folding knife, walked over, bent down, and stabbed his rear tire. It deflated immediately. That got him pissed and out of the car. I snapped another picture of him as he came for me, but I jumped back in the Suburban and threw it in gear. He took a swipe at my rear fender as I took off, leaving him sucking my fumes.

"So long, sucker," I said smiling to myself .

CHAPTER 13

I drove to a bar on Lincoln Boulevard, one that advertises Turtle Racing, and that I knew would be open this early. It had a lot out back where I could park out of sight. It would be pretty quiet this time of day, and I needed a place where I could sit and think. I ordered an early lunch and nursed a beer while I tried to figure out how I could find out who Mustang Man was. The place was empty except for some old salt at the other end of the bar, obviously a regular, and the bored tattooed, butch barmaid who was trying to ignore his drunken banter while she texted away on her phone. The old salt reminded me of myself, or what I might turn into after another twenty-five or thirty years living like I was.

I thought about calling Detective Gomez, but I didn't want to bring any more attention to myself from the police by asking him to check a license plate number. Instead, I tried my auto insurance company. I told the agent who picked up that I think I may have been a victim of a hit-and-run. I made up a story that my car got hit while parked, and someone took down the license plate number for me. But the woman on the phone said no. She said I would have to make a claim and press charges in order to get the registration info from the police.

"You understand. A lot of people try to get information on people for nefarious reasons," the insurance agent explained.

"Guess I never thought of that," I replied.

She told me I had to call the police anyway to get an accident report for filing a claim, but unless I was pressing charges they probably wouldn't be any help tracking down the license plate number. I told her I'd do that and hung up when she asked me for my policy number.

Who else could get me that info? A lawyer? Probably. Pichter? Sure, but I wasn't going to call him. Then I remembered something that had struck me as strange at the time, last night on the way home in his car, but I'd forgotten about it. How did Jonathan Pichter know about the money Pays Lee was carrying back from Vegas the night he was killed? He knew the exact amount, or at least the ballpark figure. He was the one that said it was upwards of eight hundred thousand. And didn't Rudy say he'd driven Pays over to Pichter's office on occasion. Rudy said Pichter was Pays' attorney and was bringing in investors who didn't want to be associated with Pays or the whole gangsta rap scene, but knew a good investment when they saw it. Could this money have been some under the table "investment" arranged by Pichter?

Or was Pays blackmailing Pichter over those pictures of Lauren? Blackmail? Does that make sense? Seems it would be just as dangerous for Pays if those photos got out—him with an underage girl. But what if it were blackmail or some kind of payoff? What if Pays got Pichter to pay him hush money in the sum of eight hundred thousand while he was in Vegas? Would that have pushed Pichter to have Pays killed over it? Would seeing those pictures of Lauren and Pays be enough for Pichter to want him dead? If so, why would he pay him if he was going to have him killed? And how did Rudy play into all this?

What the hell was I thinking? Do people *really* have people killed? I could see something like that happening back in New York, but here? In the papers, I'd seen the mob hits there. I even grew up with a few mobsters-on-the-fringe, bookies, and thieves. Guys who had alliances to crews. Guys who were connected. "Cheesecake Racketeers," we used to call them. But this was L.A.! La La Land. Jonathan Pichter? Was it possible? He was certainly powerful enough. And stranger things have gone down here in Tinseltown.

This was all beginning to sound like some wild, hair-brained conspiracy theory movie. Pays, Omar, and Rudy were all murdered, that was for sure. As I went over all this in my head, trying to make sense out of it, I remembered something else. I dug out a business card from my wallet. Morris Bigsby, the criminal attorney. Yeah. I wonder how much he knows? He's got to be pretty close to Pichter to be dragged out on a Sunday night on short notice to bail me out. Maybe he could shed some light on things. I didn't know how, but I dialed his number.

"Hello, can I speak to Mister Bigsby?" I asked the receptionist.

"May I ask who's calling?" she asked.

"Michael Millek."

"And may I ask what this is in reference to?"

"He'll know," I said, hoping he'd pick up after she put me on hold. The old salt had ordered another round and was toasting the barmaid when the receptionist got back on the line.

"Mister Bigsby is in a meeting right now and asked me to take a message," she said.

Meetings! Everybody in this town is always in a fucking meeting. It was a bullshit way of saying I don't want to talk to you, leave a message, and I'll see if I deem you worthy enough to call back. I told the receptionist I could hold but she said it might be a while. Another way of saying he's never going to take your call.

"Tell him"—I reached for the straws—"I may know where Mister Pichter could locate his lost item," I said before giving her my number and hanging up.

I was still trying to figure out how to play this and what I was going to tell Bigsby when my phone rang. I recognized the number—Bigsby's.

"Mister Bigsby, thank you for calling me back so soon," I answered.

"So, Mister Millek, I take it you were not entirely truthful last night when you told Mister Pichter you were not in possession of the items you had mentioned?"

"Oh, no, I was truthful about that," I lied. "I'm talking about the money he paid to Pays Lee that was supposed to end up with the man in the Mustang that's been following me since last night."

"I'm sorry, I don't follow you," he said.

I gave Bigsby the Mustang's plate number and told him when he found out who it belonged to call me back, and he might want to let Pichter know.

"This is all very cloak and dagger, Mister Millek."

"I believe the money was a payment made to Pays Lee for keeping quiet about some incriminating photos of Jonathan Pichter's daughter. It was subsequently to be collected by the man in the Mustang when he killed Pays Lee. Only he didn't collect it, and I believe he thinks I have it. So he's been stalking my place and following me. I would like it to stop."

"Hold on a second, Mister Millek. Let me get this straight. You think that some mystery man, in a Mustang, was hired by Mister Pichter to kill Pays Lee?"

"Something like that" I said. There was silence on the line until...

"Mister Millek, do you realize the implications of the claim you are making? Please take my advice. Forget this paranoid delusion of yours, and please, cease and desist in calling Mister Pichter or myself ever again. I can assure you it will not work out well for you if you don't."

"Now hold on, Mister Fancy Pants," and figuring I had nothing left to lose at this point, I let him have it. "I may not be some swinging-dick Beverly Hills client of yours, but I'm not just blowing paranoid smoke up your ass, okay? Besides that dirt-bag Pays Lee, my best friend was murdered Saturday night too. You know the cops are trying to blame me. But it was Pichter who told me Pays Lee was carrying a large amount of cash. Eight hundred thousand to be exact, that was the number he mentioned. And he no doubt thinks I have it for some stupid reason because I was the one who discovered their dead bodies. My guess is he's trying get his money back and has this guy in the Mustang following me to get it. So when I tell you I'm being stalked and followed, possibly by a murderer, and probably because of Jonathan Pichter, I would appreciate it if you took me seriously. So please discuss this with Mister Pichter and get me that license plate info. Otherwise I will personally create a media shitstorm that will put your client in a very bright spotlight that I am sure he does not want to be in."

The line went quiet again as Bigsby put this all together. Threatening to go to the media got his attention.

"Look, I'm not trying to be a threat to you or Pichter. I'm simply trying to keep my own ass safe here. Get me that info on the Mustang, and I'll be happy to cut you and Pichter out of the loop," I told him.

"Let me call you back, Mister Millek," he sighed.

"Thank you, Mister Bigsby."

"I hope you know what you're getting yourself in for," he said.

"I'm beginning to get a pretty good idea," I told him before I hung up.

I was betting a lot on what I'd told him. I didn't know if any of it was true, but it was definitely plausible. Either way, I was going to find out who Mustang Man was and find out if he was Rudy's murderer.

Being charged up by what I had put together and my call to Bigsby, I threw caution to the wind and decided to pay a visit to the Santa Monica P.D. to see if I could get my guns back. I didn't like the idea of where this all was going, being in the middle of all of it and not packing any protection. I dialed Rick Gomez's number.

"Robbery Homicide," but it was Detective Lo that answered the phone.

"Hi, Lo." I almost laughed at the way that sounded. "It's Mike Millek. How's it going?"

"Millek! You ready to give me your confession?" he asked.

"Put your rubber hose away, Lo. I already told you I have nothing to confess."

"Okay, tough guy. If you say so. But you're digging yourself deeper."

"You know, if you just did your job, maybe you would find the killer," I said.

"Don't worry, we'll find him...and the money!"

That made me think of Ari Goldman fucking his ingénue aboard *Above the Line*. Yeah, good luck, Lo, I thought.

"Well, I'm happy to hear that. In the meantime, when can I pick up my confiscated firearms?"

"Why do you need them? You got more people to shoot?"

"Look, I've got a perfectly legal conceal carry permit for the State of California and the County of Los Angeles. I have every right to be in possession of those firearms. Or should I have my lawyer call your boss?"

"They're at the ballistics lab. They're part of an ongoing criminal investigation. When they're cleared, you can pick them up."

"And when's that going to be?" I asked.

"I don't know, Millek. They said they were very backlogged," he said smugly.

The other line on my phone was ringing. It was Bigsby.

"Backlogged, huh? I guess I'll have to call you back." I hung up and took Bigsby's call.

"Mister Millek."

"Yes, Mister Bigsby."

"I have some news for you," he said. "It seems that plate number is registered to a Ms. Catherine Charles, age seventy-eight, of Yuba City, California. And the car is a 2002 Mercury Marquis."

"I see." Damn, I thought. Stolen plates. Now what?

"So, if there won't be anything else, Mister Millek, I wish

you all the..."

"Hold it," I said remembering the pictures. "What's your email address?"

"I hardly think we have anything else to..."

"Listen to me! I've got a couple of pictures of the guy. I'm going to email them to you, and you're going to show them to Pichter, and get me a name."

"Mister Millek, please..."

"And if I don't hear back from you with a name by the end of the day, I'll be going to the media and the police, and telling them all about what was on Lauren Bartley's phone."

Bigsby gave me his email address before asking, "And what if Mister Pichter cannot identify this mystery man?"

"I'm betting he will," I said and hung up.

I drafted a quick email, attached the photos of Mustang Man and sent it to Bigsby.

The barmaid came over and asked if I wanted another round as I downed the last of my now warm beer. I told her no thanks, threw a twenty down, and told her to keep the change. As I got up to leave, the old salt waved goodbye.

"Fair winds and following seas to you, matey," he said.

"Aye-aye, and to you as well, Captain," I saluted.

CHAPTER 14

I didn't want to head home in case Mustang Man was back there waiting for me. I needed a couple of things in order to get the money off of Ari's boat, so I headed back over to the marina to Ship's Supply, a local chandlery shop. There I grabbed a suitcase-sized waterproof Pelican roller case, some half-inch braided line, a new Danforth anchor, and some oil-absorbent cloths. Maybe my paranoia was getting the best of me, but I paid in cash just in case someone was watching my credit card purchases or if things went south.

Next up, I had to figure out how to get my canvas tool bag out of my dock box. I decided to park the Suburban over in the C Basin near Ari's boat so I could come back and keep an eye on it. Luckily, Ari's fifteen-year-old Rolls Royce, parked nearby, was easy to spot. So I had no doubt Ari was still aboard *Above the Line*, banging his sexy Israeli starlet. So much for discretion, I thought.

I took the Pelican case and the anchor out and wheeled them over via the pedestrian path to B Basin, Tiki Marina and *Stella*. I crept up and kept my eyes out for Mustang Man or any sign of him. There didn't appear to be any, so I headed down my dock to *Stella* with the suitcase and anchor. I hopped aboard and opened her up as fast as I could. While below, I peered out my portholes, again scanning the area for any signs of him. I didn't see anything out of the ordinary, but still had that uneasy feeling, like I was being watched.

After stashing the Pelican case and the anchor up in the V-berth, I hopped back out on the dock and retrieved my canvas tool bag from my dock box. I carried it aboard *Stella* and went below again. The canvas tool bag was the biggest one I could find when I bought it and it served me well, holding pretty much all of my hand tools and whatever power tool I might need for a particular jib. I emptied it out, laying out my tools on the settee table then replaced the couple I thought I would need for the job. Satisfied and sweaty, I went on deck and locked up *Stella,* tool bag in hand. Trying to be nonchalant about it, I tossed my tool bag into my inflatable dinghy and hopped aboard. I hadn't used the dinghy in some time, and I didn't want to take the chance of the motor not starting, sputtering and drawing attention to myself. So instead, I untied the dock line and quickly rowed away. When I got about halfway down the basin, I took a chance and pulled the starter cord. The engine came to life on the third pull, and after a quick warm-up, I motored over to C Basin, and *Above the Line.*

I tied up at the end of the dock, as I had earlier with Peter Darcy's dinghy. I grabbed my tool bag, walked over to the parking area and put it in my Suburban. I settled in behind the wheel and kept my eyes peeled on *Above the Line.* Ari's Rolls was still parked in the same spot. I figured he was going to have to get off that boat sooner or later. After about an hour of checking emails and deleting junk off my phone, I sat back and closed my eyes. The last couple of days had been a whirlwind without much sleep, and it was catching up to me. I must have dosed off into a deep sleep because I was jolted awake by my phone ringing. My phone told me I was out for over an hour and that the caller was Bigsby.

"Hello?" I said trying my best not to sound like I just woke up.

"Mister Millek, I have a name for you," he said.

I tried to snap to, and I grabbed a pen and my pad from the console.

"Looks like I was correct."

"The name is Ernesto Swanzy," Bigsby said.

"Ernesto Swanzy," I repeated writing it down. The name sounded vaguely familiar. "So who is Ernesto Swanzy?"

"You asked me to get you a name, Mister Millek. I did. I trust you will keep up your end of the bargain. And I would advise you not to go to the police with it."

"Why not?" I asked, still trying to focus.

"I think you know why. Good day to you, sir," and with that, he hung up.

Okay, what the hell did that mean? I thought to myself, still trying to shake loose the cobwebs in my brain. Who the hell is Ernesto Swanzy? Why did that name sound familiar? And how was I going to find out? Why did he tell me not to go to the police? I was about to Google the name on my phone when another call came in. This time it was Molly.

"Hey, how's it going?" I answered, still a little groggy.

"How are you doing? You sound awful," she said.

"I must have fallen asleep," I said. I suddenly remembered where I was and took a quick look around. Ari's Rolls was still there.

"Well, we're wrapping up here for the day. You still want me to come over?"

My head was in a fog but the thought of seeing Molly perked me up.

"Sure. That sounds great—" I suddenly thought of Mustang Man, now known as Ernesto Swanzy. I got a little more paranoid about him, now that I knew his name. He might be back at Tiki Marina by now, waiting for me.

"Actually, Molly, I was wondering, could I come over to your place?" I asked.

I used the excuse that my place was still a mess from the police tearing it apart and that I hadn't had a chance to straighten up. I think she could sense that something was amiss but she agreed.

"Is everything okay, Mike?" she asked.

"Yeah, sure. I...look, I'll fill you in when I see you, okay?" I promised.

"Okay. See you in a bit."

I think Molly felt funny about having me over to her place, the home she shared with Jimmy. I sat for a moment after getting off the phone with her. My inflatable was still tied to the end of Ari's dock. I figured I could leave it there for the night. Molly would no doubt have an early call time so I'd be back here in time to move it before the dock master got in. Plus it would give me a way to get back to Tiki Marina without driving the Suburban there in case Mustang Man Ernesto was there.

I decided Ari would not be leaving any time soon, maybe not for the rest of the night, so I headed over to Molly's. She lived in Laurel Canyon, and I knew it would take a while in early evening rush hour traffic. As I drove across town on Venice Boulevard, I Googled Ernesto Swanzy, reading the results as I crawled in traffic and stopped at red lights. By time I got to Sepulveda Boulevard, I had my answer. Ernesto Swanzy was one of Michelle Bartley's bodyguards back in the day when the diva was going through her drug scandal. After she went into rehab, he actually made the news as one of her enablers, acquiring and supplying her with crack cocaine. I stumbled across an old article in the *L.A. Times* where he was fingered for contributing to her downfall. He fought the allegations and eventual charges by saying he was just doing what he was told to by his employer. He was legally exonerated but held accountable in the court of public opinion. So here was a connection to Michelle Bartley and by association, Jonathan Pichter. That must have been why Bixby warned me about going to the police.

I was still trying to put it all together as I pulled into a market off Sunset. I picked up a bottle of wine to take to Molly, and as an afterthought, I grabbed a nice little flower arrangement as well. At this point I was really hoping I could turn my mind off and enjoy a nice evening with Molly. I also thought that bouncing some of what I learned off someone else might help me see things I'd missed. Molly was a good listener, a good friend, and I trusted her implicitly. She knew what was going on, to some extent. And she knew Rudy. Perhaps she could give me a new perspective or shed some light in the murky corners of this whole affair. I decided I would fill her in on everything that was going on—with the exception to my taking the money of course.

When I got to Molly's, she seemed a little reserved. She didn't greet me with the open arms I was hoping for. I again chalked it up to me being in the house she shared with Jimmy. She thanked me for the flowers, and I followed her into the kitchen so she could put them in water. We made small talk about her day on the location set and what was going on with the film. I told her about my conversation with Sandy and Rudy's sister. It had been some time since I'd been to the house, but I noticed that she had taken down all the photos and reminders of her and Jimmy's life together from around the house. I commented on how good the house looked.

"Thanks. Realtor called me this morning," she perked up. "She wants to do a showing this weekend."

"Oh, yeah? That's good, right?" I asked.

"Probably. She wants to put it on the market for one point five. That's almost three times the amount we paid for it."

"One point five? Wow, you're like rich!" I teased her.

"Well, I'm still going to have to split some of it with the weasel," she said, referring to Jimmy. "But I'm not going to make it easy for him. I got one helluva divorce lawyer."

"Hell hath no fury like a woman scorned."

"Damn right," she replied.

Once the flowers were in a vase, the wine opened, and glasses poured, we went outside and sat in the garden. Molly had done a great job of transforming the small barren backyard at the bottom of the hillside into a beautiful garden with a comfortable sitting area. We took a seat next to each other on a cozy, teak garden bench. The scent of night blooming jasmine filled the air.

As we settled in, she finally turned to me and asked straight out, "So, what's going on, Mike?"

I took a deep breath, leaned in and started to spill everything. I started off by recapping my professional relationship with Pays Lee. Then I brought her up to date with what had transpired with Lauren the last time I had picked him up.

"She was the one you wanted clothes for that day you came to the studio?" she asked.

"Exactly."

I went on about how Lauren had disappeared by time I got back to *Stella*, how I later found her phone in the Suburban, and discovered who exactly she was.

"Michelle Bartley's daughter?! Oh my god! I worked on that Bessie Wallace movie with Michelle. I remember her daughter. She was only around two back then. She was adorable."

"Yeah, well, she blossomed pretty nicely." I told her about the photos and video I found on her phone.

"With Pays Lee?! A fifteen-year-old! That is disgusting!"

I agreed, skipping over the part about me making copies to protect myself, but laying out Rudy at Pays' office and Carl a.k.a. Khakis Sport Jacket, and how he played soccer on my ribs when he came to get Lauren's phone back. She remembered the bruises. I told her turns out Carl is a "security consultant," or bodyguard, to Pichter and Michelle Bartley. Molly sat there sipping her wine, intrigued by my story and piecing it together by asking questions on details that needed filling in.

After refilling our glasses, I told Molly about Pays Lee's last call and the texted money photo to get me to pick him up. And since I knew Pays Lee owed Rudy money too that I called him to give him a heads-up but could only leave a message.

She stopped me when I got to my arrival at the airport, asking, "Wait, Jonathan Pichter's bodyguard took Lauren's phone from you, with all those compromising pictures and videos of their daughter, and the next time you see Pays Lee, he's dead? Murdered?"

"Yeah."

"Don't you see? I mean it sounds pretty obvious that they—Jonathan Pichter or Michelle Bartley or both of them—had Pays Lee killed! I mean, they have motive if they saw those pictures, don't you think?" she hypothesized. "Hell, I would have had him killed if he had done that to my daughter."

I thought about Swanzy and what Bigsby said about going to the police. It was starting to make sense.

"Yeah, well, that's kind of what I was thinking. But I guess I couldn't put my mind around somebody doing that. Having someone killed, I mean."

"Mike, didn't you tell this to the police?"

I tried to explain that since I didn't have any proof, it sounded like too wild of a story, and I didn't think they would believe me. But Molly wasn't having it. "You need to go to the police."

"Before you make any judgments or tell me what I should do..."

"But Mike—"

"Please! Hear me out. And *then* I want to hear what you have to say. Everything, and your advice," I said.

So she sat back and I continued my story: what transpired at the police station after our sailing outing; how I bluffed Pichter into thinking I had a copy of the photos and video; and how he'd sent a criminal attorney to get me out.

"Don't you see? That just proves it," she said.

"Hold on," I said, "What about the ride home I got from Pichter and Carl?" I told her about the amount of money Pichter mentioned that Pays Lee was holding and how he seemed to know the exact amount. I let that sink in while I sipped my wine.

"How would he know, unless..." She looked at me.

"Unless he had something to do with that money," I said in agreement.

"But why? I mean, I still think it's highly likely that he had Pays killed, but…"

"I don't know," I said, shaking my head. "Rudy mentioned Pichter lining up silent investors—maybe that something to do with it? The cops knew he was carrying cash but I don't think they knew the amount. They saw the picture Pays Lee texted me. And who knows, maybe they heard it from Pays Lee's crew or someone saw it in Vegas."

"Didn't you tell me those rapper guys were always ripping each other off?" she asked.

I nodded.

"So whoever ripped him off, killed them. Right?"

"Makes sense." I didn't look her in the eyes. "But that still doesn't answer the question of how Jonathan Pichter knew about the money."

"Well, could be like you said. He arranged some silent investor," she said. "Or…"

"Or what?"

"What if Jonathan Pichter arranged for Pays Lee to receive the money from a so-called silent investor. Then—I know this is going to sound crazy, but…" she said becoming animated like she was on to something.

"No, go ahead. It's all freakin' crazy," I told her.

"What if the money was really a payoff for the killer, the hit man? So, you know, it all looks like a robbery."

I pondered this, happy to hear it come out of Molly's mouth since this had passed through my mind as well. Maybe I wasn't crazy for thinking it. Or maybe we were both crazy. The big question now was, why didn't the killer take the money? But I couldn't say that to Molly.

"Rudy!" I blurted out.

"What? You think Rudy had something to with this?" she asked.

"No, I'm trying to figure out why he got killed as well," I said covering myself. But I tried to put it together as simply as I could, thinking out loud. "Because Rudy showed up unexpectedly. He wasn't supposed to be there. I'd left him a message but I didn't leave any details. Pays Lee must have called him for a ride too. I gave him shit on the phone..."

"Rudy?"

"No, Pays Lee. Maybe he didn't think I was going to show, so he called Rudy for a ride. I got there late on purpose to make Pays sweat for stiffing me for so long. Rudy must have shown up on time. And got killed for it." Then it struck me. "Shit! It could have been..."

Molly placed her wine glass down, put her arms around me, and whispered my name. We hugged tightly. I pushed her back to arms' length, looked her in the eyes, and asked her flat out, "Was it my fault? Rudy?"

"Mike...don't even go there."

I pulled her in close again. It felt good to hold her. It felt good to be held by her. It felt good to open up to her, to talk things out, get things off my chest. Somehow I knew it would help and it did.

It was her turn to pull away. We looked into each other's eyes. We both had tears in them, but there was a connection, a deep connection. Far more than sexual, it was an intense, penetrating human bond. We hugged again, holding on tightly, embracing each other like our lives depended on it, until our lips met and we kissed. We kissed each other deeply and as our passion grew, we held each other tight, caressing each other, lips exploring. I nuzzled my face into her hair, breathing her in, chest swelling, breathing her inside me.

"Let's go inside," she whispered in my ear.

We stood up and I lifted her in my arms, cradling her. She held me tight and buried her face in my chest. I carried her inside the house to her bedroom. I laid her gently down on the bed, and we undressed each other, our lips meeting in tender kisses, tongues searching, our hunger growing. Once naked, we lay together on the bed, gently caressing, our bodies pressing, entwining, and finally joining. Finding each other's rhythm, we moved connected, together as one. We made a deep unbound and uninhibited yet tender love. Climaxing together in a primeval, seemingly ceaseless ecstasy, we held on to each other tightly, neither of us wanting to let go. We were one.

We caught our breaths and kissed tenderly in the afterglow. I brushed Molly's hair away from her face, and we looked deep into each other's eyes. No words needed to be said. I felt like I was experiencing the purest form of love I had ever felt. This was way beyond the best sex I'd ever had. This was on a whole other level. It wasn't just lust. It was a human bond that I had never felt before.

Suddenly I felt open and vulnerable, self-conscious and full of doubts, because I wasn't sure—though I hoped—Molly was feeling the same. But she smiled with a look of warm contentment before she snuggled her face into my shoulder. I nuzzled her thick, luscious, strawberry blond locks, drinking in the pleasure I felt by having her so close. I didn't want this to ever end. *If I were to die right now*, I thought, *I would die a happy man, having now felt what real, true love was like.*

We awoke the next morning in each other's arms when the alarm went off at 4:00 a.m. We cursed the world of reality as we kissed and reluctantly jumped out of bed. We showered together, trying very hard to not get too aroused to distract us from getting ready to leave. Molly had to get to work, and I wanted to get back to the marina. Somehow, I had to get that money. As coffee brewed and we dressed, Molly told me she was happy I'd come by last night. I told her I was too. I should have stopped right there, but I let my usual guard down—I told her I thought it was probably the best night of my life. I instantly regretted saying it, and I felt like a total fool. She stopped putting her earrings in, turned, and looked at me, smiling brightly. After a moment, she said, "You don't have to say that."

"I'm sorry, that must have sounded like quite the line."

"Did you mean it?" she asked.

"I've never said anything like that to any woman before," I said, somewhat embarrassed. I saw the way she was looking at me. "But, yeah, I did. I meant every word of it."

She came over to me, looking for the truth in my eyes. Seeing it, she caressed my cheek and planted a gentle kiss on my lips before telling me, "I feel the same way, Mike."

My heart filled with happiness. We went to the kitchen and decided to sit for a minute over coffee before heading out. She asked me what I was going to do about the whole Pays Lee situation, if I was going to tell the police the theory we came up with. What transpired the previous night had made me forget all about it, and now I wanted to tell her everything.

"There's more." I filled her in about being followed by Mustang Man, getting his info, and losing him by giving him a flat. And how I threatened Pichter's criminal attorney with going to the media if he didn't get me Mustang Man's identity.

"Ernesto Swanzy?" she asked. "Why does that name sound familiar?"

I told her what I learned.

"Right! Ernie, we called him. He was around on the Bessie Wallace show! You think he could be the killer?"

"That's what I aim to find out," I told her.

"You need to go to the police with *all* of this."

"I will. Just as soon as I can prove it to them."

"Wait...do you think he could have followed you here?"

"No way. I haven't seen him since I gave him that flat tire," I reassured her. "But that's why I didn't want you coming over to my place. He might still me staking me out."

She was digesting all this new info when she looked at her watch and realized it was time to go. I walked her out to her Prius and kissed her goodbye. She held me at arm's length and looked me in the eyes.

"Mike, promise me you'll go to the police and talk to them."

"I will. When I can tell them something without sounding like a paranoid lunatic," I said.

"Even paranoid people have something to be scared of, you know."

I laughed, as she got in her car and started it up. She rolled her window down and asked, "Will I see you tonight?"

"I sure hope so." I smiled warmly. "I'll make sure it's safe over at my place if you want to come over there."

"Okay. Can we sleep on your boat?" she asked.

This took me by surprise, and I laughed. "Why?"

"I've never slept on a sailboat. I think it would be romantic."

"Sure. Whatever you want."

We exchanged small waves as she backed out of the driveway and headed down the hill. I watched her go, then got in the Suburban, trying to figure out what my next move was going to be.

CHAPTER 15

First thing I wanted to do was to get over to the marina and check on Ari Goldman's boat. I was formulating a plan to get on board, but it meant going back to Tiki Marina and grabbing my wetsuit off of *Stella*. That meant parking at Ari's marina where I left my dinghy and taking it back over to B Basin and Tiki Marina to avoid Swanzy if he was there. I had to be careful. I felt getting to *Stella* via my inflatable was still the best bet for getting in and out of there unseen.

At the C Basin marina, I saw that Ari's Rolls was still in the same spot so I parked a good distance away but where I could still keep my eye on it. I crept down to my dinghy at the end of his dock. It was pretty early, the sun was trying to make its way over the buildings, and I didn't want to wake up Ari or any of the other live-aboards on the dock. I hopped in and rowed all the way down to the main channel before starting the outboard and cruising over to B Basin. When I got about halfway down B Basin, I killed the engine and rowed the rest of the way to *Stella*. I scanned the marina—no sign of the Mustang, Swanzy, or anything that looked out of place. Tying up to *Stella* I climbed aboard and retrieved my wetsuit, mask, and snorkel from the wet locker. I stripped down and squeezed into the wetsuit before I threw my clothes and a towel into a backpack I keep aboard. Then I opened my engine compartment and grabbed the used oil absorbent pads from under the engine in my bilge and replaced them with the new ones I'd bought the previous day. Throwing them in a plastic bag along with a screwdriver, I stuffed them in the backpack as well. I had another look around from the companionway before closing up *Stella* and jumping back into my inflatable. I rowed away quietly until I was far enough to pull the starter cord and motored back over to C Basin.

This time I tied up to the stern of one Ari's neighbors. I knew the guy, and he rarely came down to his forty-two foot Hunter sailboat, and when he did, it was always on the weekend. I donned my mask and snorkel and dug out the plastic bag with the oil-soaked pads and screwdriver before slipping over the side into the murky marina water. I made my way over to *Above the Line* and popped my head up on the starboard side near one of the bilge pump exhaust outlets. I took the oily rags from the bag and stuffed them tightly into the narrow, round vent. I shoved the clump in further with the end of the screwdriver, making sure it wasn't visible from outside.

I swam under the boat to the port side and was about to do the same to this side when the automatic bilge pump kicked on and spit a mouthful of bilge water into my face. I gagged and thought I was going to puke as I spit it out, reeling from the putrid taste and hoping I didn't make too much noise for anyone aboard to notice. I recovered finally and stuffed another oily pad into the outlet's mouth, completely plugging it. My hope was that these pads would back-up the bilge enough for the bilge alarm to go off which would cause Ari to call me.

Mission accomplished. I climbed back into the dinghy, grabbed the backpack, and headed to the boaters' restroom. I let myself in, got out of the wetsuit, and showered off the toxic marina water. I let the water rinse out my mouth, but still couldn't get rid of the foul taste.

Once dressed, I walked back over to the Suburban and threw my wetsuit and backpack in the way-back next to my tool bag. I settled in behind the wheel and kept an eye on Ari's boat. I was sure Ari and his ingénue had spent the night, which made me think about my night with Molly. I relived every moment in my head. It almost made me forget about the money, as if I had another priority now. Almost. Because I knew that money would buy me some freedom to do a lot with Molly. I fantasized about the two of us sailing away on *Stella* with plenty in the coffers to keep us going for a very long time.

My thoughts turned back to Mustang Swanzy. Was he staking out my place? Or maybe he got rid of the Mustang and was driving something different so I wouldn't notice him. Was he really the killer? All the signs were pointing to him. Then the big question: should I go to the police with the info I had about him? It could be a big risk, what with Pichter's veiled threat delivered via Bigsby. My ribs still hurt, and they twinged at the thought of dealing with Carl again. Would the police even believe me? And would they protect me if they did? Pichter was a Hollywood power broker. I was just some below-the-line movie teamster. All these questions ran through my head, but I kept coming back to Molly, remembering how right it felt to be wrapped up in her arms.

I wanted to wait until mid-morning before I called Chris DeLuca about coming back to work. I didn't want to bother him too early in the morning when I knew things on location would be hectic. It was around 8:00 a.m. and still no sign of any activity on Ari's yacht when my phone rang. It was Molly.

"He knows," was all she said.

"What? Who?"

"Jimmy. He knows you spent the night. He confronted me about it, so I told him the truth."

My heart sunk. I wished I hadn't heard what Molly had said. I still considered Jimmy a friend and even though their marriage was over, I knew he wouldn't take kindly to someone he knows sleeping with his ex.

"Was he upset?" I asked cautiously.

"He made a total scene. I couldn't believe it. He ruins our marriage by screwing some twenty-four-year-old P.A., and now

141

he's giving me shit for spending the night with you."

"What'd he say?"

"He went into this whole rant. 'How could you?' I told him it was pretty easy after what he'd done to me."

This wasn't sounding good, and my head started pounding. "So, how did it end?"

"Oh, you know, the usual. He stormed off, cursing, telling me he was going to get me fired from the show. His usual bruised male ego bravado."

I pictured the scene, trying to let it all sink in. "Are you okay?"

"Yeah, I guess..."

"Are you worried?"

"About what?" she asked.

"Losing the gig."

"No. Not really. Jane wouldn't let him fire me." Jane Goodward was the show's costume designer, in charge of Molly's department and her immediate boss.

"But at this point I don't really care. It was probably a bad idea working on this picture with him to begin with. Now the thought of working with him for the next twelve weeks, with him being an asshole..." She let that hang.

"How did he find out?" I finally asked.

Molly said she wasn't sure, but he may have come by and seen my Suburban parked outside their house. Jimmy had been known to "drop by" unannounced to collect something from the house that he'd left or forgotten.

"He's living in the valley and drives through the canyon on his way to the studio," she explained. "If he saw your car last night, he may have swung by in the morning to see if it was still there."

"Jeez," was all I could say, exasperated.

Another call came in. I checked the ID and saw it was Chris Deluca. This must be my pink slip. I let it go to voicemail, figuring I'd wait to hear the bad news. My head was starting to throb even more.

"Are you mad?" she asked.

"No, no. It's not the way I would have liked him to find out. But what's done is done. I sure as hell don't regret last night."

"Neither do I." I could hear the smile in her voice. "We're still on for tonight, right?"

"Absolutely," I replied. "You know it's going to piss him off even more if he swings by your place tonight and doesn't see your car there."

"I know. Good!"

We laughed and said our goodbyes.

When I hung up, I rubbed my temples and braced myself for Chris' message. But all he said was "Call me."

As I punched the reply button, I prepared myself for the worst. He picked up after a couple of rings.

"Mike."

"Chris."

"What the fuck?" was all he asked.

"What can I say?"

"You know Jimmy wants you off the show."

"I figured as much. No way to go to bat for me?" I asked as a last-ditch effort.

"I'm sorry, Mike. My hands are tied. He said if you don't go, he's going to replace the whole department."

"Can he do that? I mean with the union…"

"He can fire whoever he wants. If we fight it, he can make up any bullshit excuse, and then we'll all be blackballed."

"Shit. I'm sorry, Chris."

"Hey, it just sucks, dude. Especially after this whole thing with Rudy."

"Yeah…my own fault, I guess."

Chris told me he'd mail my check because he didn't think it would be a good idea to show my face at set. I agreed, at least not until Jimmy cooled down. Chris told me he'd keep an ear out for me with our brother teamsters for any leads on other shows. I thanked him before hanging up. I was really going to need that stashed cash now that I lost my job. I glanced over at Ari's boat and wondered how much fucking this guy could do before coming up for air. I couldn't believe he hadn't left the boat yet. All I could do was wait and hope my bilge plugs would work. And that he'd call me as soon as the alarm went off.

I was getting tired of doing the stakeout, and my head was still killing me, so I decided to sneak back to my place. I walked over to the Tiki Marina apartment building, and there was no sign of Swanzy. I approached cautiously, scanning the area and all the parked cars as I circled the building. As I approached a side entrance, I ran into Liz Blanco.

She said, "Someone's looking for you."

My heart froze. "What? When?"

"Yesterday. He was hanging around, loitering, so I asked if I there was something I could help him with," she said. "He said he was looking for you, that he wanted to check out your boat. He said it was for sale. Are you selling it?"

I gave my standard answer that if someone offered the price I was asking then of course it's for sale. Then I inquired about the man. "What'd he look like?" I asked figuring he probably didn't give a name.

Liz described Swanzy to a tee. I asked if she'd seen him since.

"No, I told him he couldn't wait around and that he needed to call you to set up an appointment to see your boat."

I apologized to her and told her that I had an ad in *The Log*, a local boating rag, but that he never called. Better to get rid of the guy.

"But you know, let me know if he shows up again," I told her. "Give me a call."

"I will," she said, then added, "You're not really going to sell your boat, are you? After all you put into it?"

"I am starting to rethink the idea. But everything has its price."

"Well, if you do, be sure to tell whoever buys it that the slip is *not* part of the deal. I'm always finding out tenants sell their boats and the new owners think that they can take over the slip."

I told her not to worry, I knew the score. I'd heard her bitch about this problem before. Boat owners are notorious for selling their boats and telling the buyers that the slip is included, when in fact it was never theirs to offer.

It was a relief to hear that Liz chased off Swanzy. She always tries to keep the place safe and scandal-free, but that meant he was probably keeping an eye out in some other way. I casually looked around to see if he was watching us now.

"So what happened over the weekend, with all the cops in your place?" Liz doesn't work on the weekends so I had to explain about the Pays Lee shooting, and how I discovered the bodies.

"Wow, I heard about that on the news. It was you that found his body?"

I told her that because I was the first on the scene, the cops thought I might have had something to do with it, and how they ransacked my place and the boat looking for clues.

"Obviously they didn't find anything," I told her, hoping to relieve her concern.

"Did they arrest you?"

"They took me in for further questioning because they couldn't find anything. They thought they could sweat a confession out of me."

"Weren't you nervous?" she asked.

"A bit, I guess. It's not what you might call fun, when the cops haul you down to the station house."

"Wow. So they still don't know who did it?"

I sure didn't want to tell Liz that it was probably the guy she chased off yesterday, so I just said, "Nope," then changed the subject by asking her about her own boat. She said she and her husband were having some problems with the engine. It was an old four-cylinder Palmer. I offered to take a look at it when I had a chance. She thanked me and went on her way, and I continued up to my apartment.

My place was still a mess. After popping three Advils and

washing them down with some orange juice that was way past the expiration date, I went straight for *Moby Dick* and confirmed the thumb drive was still there. Next, I went to the window and peered out the blinds, trying to figure out where I would be if I were spying on my place. My answer: either in one of the boats in the basin, which I ruled out due to Liz and the security gates or on the roof of the building across the basin. It was almost a quarter of a mile away, so if someone were there, they would need some good binoculars. I looked through the shambles that was now my apartment and finally found my binoculars. I scanned the building across the way, checking both rooftop and balconies. No sign of Swanzy. I was now thinking that maybe I should not have given him that flat tire. Maybe it would have been better to have him on my tail so at least I knew where he was. Better than having him out there somewhere and not knowing where. Because I was sure he *was* out there, waiting for me, somewhere.

I spent over an hour straightening up my place, constantly checking my phone to see if Ari had called. I was hoping his bilge would be backing up by now. But it was hard to predict. Sitting at the dock is not conducive to filling one's bilge, especially on a boat as nicely maintained as *Above the Line*. Maybe it was time for Plan B. The trouble was I didn't have a Plan B yet, other than going and knocking on his door. I'd have to come up with some story to get him off the boat for a while. Then I thought of something. I could knock and tell him I saw his wife somewhere nearby. There's a jewelry store in the marina shopping mall, and she was big on jewelry. The fact they had a house in Beverly Hills would mean that she might come down to the boat if she were in the neighborhood. She was known to bring a book and sunbathe on the deck. The thought of his wife coming down would certainly get him off for a while. As much of a bully as Ari was, he was scared of one person: his wife. Perhaps it was because she was a strong, demanding, aging Jewish Princess, or perhaps because she would no doubt take him to the cleaners if she ever found reason to divorce him.

Okay, I thought, Plan B. I headed back out. I was even more careful on the walk back to C Basin, checking every parked car along the way and every creaking boat tied to the docks. When I got to Ari's dock, I entered the security code at the gate and headed down. As I got closer, I could hear a woman's wailing cry. I slowed to a stop. Ari's girlfriend saw me through the glass and came running.

"Please! Help! Something's happened!" She was in a panic, waving me in. She wore the same silk kimono, but it was untied and she did little to hide her nakedness underneath.

I hopped aboard and ran in. I followed her down to the master stateroom, expecting to see the bilge overflowing, flooding the floor, but instead, there lying face down on the bed naked was Ari. He looked dead, and when I went to turn him over, he already felt cold and his face was blue. Adrenaline kicked in, and I immediately began performing CPR even though knew it was probably no use. Yael was backed into the corner, crying hysterically. *Well there goes Plan B*, I thought. I was going to have to improvise Plan C on the fly. Someone once told me that goals are reached by forming the right state of mind.

I jumped into command mode and barked at her. "You need to get dressed and pack all your stuff," I ordered. When she didn't move and just stood there staring at Ari, sobbing uncontrollably, I shouted, "Now!"

She had no qualms about pulling her robe off in front of me and getting dressed from her clothes in the salon closet. As I tried to figure out my next move, all I could do was look at her and think, *yeah, killer body*. Killer fuck. That's what she was. Poor Ari. Well, at least he probably went out happy.

I busied myself trying to clean things up, to make it look like Ari was here alone. I gathered glasses, champagne bottles, caviar cans, half eaten snacks, dirty dishes, and a prescription jar of Viagra the size of a pickle jar. It was half empty. I gathered most of the stuff, found a plastic trash bag, and threw it all in.

As Yael packed the last of her lotions, potions, and perfumes into her roller suitcase she said weeping, "Shouldn't we call someone?"

"We will. I mean, I will. Did you call anyone?" I suddenly panicked.

"No," she said as she shook her head.

"Good. Okay, first we've got to get you out of here," I told her. "You have any money? Credit card?"

"Some."

"Some what?" I snapped.

"Some money. A couple of credit cards," she answered.

"Okay. I'm going to take you to a nearby hotel and drop you off. You can get a room there, call someone, grab a flight home, whatever. We can't let Ari's wife and family know you were here with him," I explained.

"He's married?!" she asked, surprised.

Was she serious? Was she really *that* naïve?

"How old are you, Yael?" I asked.

"Twenty-three."

"He's got grandchildren older than you. What did you think?"

"He told me he was in love with me." She looked over her shoulder at him as I pulled her up through the salon, trash bag in tow.

"And I'm sure he meant every word of it, too."

I stopped at the door and looked around once more. I grabbed Ari's set of boat keys from the hook by the door and looked around outside before turning to Yael. She was still bawling, now confused why the man she was sleeping with for the last forty-eight hours had lied to her. I grabbed her arms and looked her in the eyes.

"Yael, listen to me. You've got to get it together and straighten up. You can't be walking out on the dock all crying and stuff. People will notice, and that is the last thing we need right now. Ari was a famous producer, and we don't want to be creating any scandals. You understand?"

She nodded, and I continued, "I'm going to take you to the hotel, it's close by, and then I'll come back and call 911. An ambulance. I'll take care of everything and leave you out of it, but you've *got* to keep it together for the next few minutes, okay? Can you do that?"

She seemed to get the picture. She wiped her eyes, took a couple of deep breaths, looked at me, and nodded. I smiled at her. She smiled back. This just might work, I thought.

I led her out, locked the boat, and carried her suitcase and the trash bag. I faked some small talk as we walked down the dock and over to my Suburban. I threw the suitcase and trash bag in the back seat and Yael got in the passenger door. I hopped in behind the wheel and complimented her on her performance. I drove her to the Marriott, the closest hotel in the marina and pulled up to the front entrance.

"Get yourself a room. Take it easy. I'll come by later and check on you, okay?" I told her.

The tears started forming again, and I reached over to her and squeezed her hand.

"It's going to be all right. You did good. Ari would be proud." I said out of lack of anything better to say.

She nodded then asked, "What about the movies he was going to put me in?"

I wanted to tell her that she should have thought about that before she fucked him to death. But instead I said, "I'm sure you'll find someone else to make them."

As I got out of the Suburban, I waved a bellman over. He walked up checking out the sexy, shapely Yael. I handed him her bag and asked him to help Yael get checked in. I explained to him that she's upset because she just learned her uncle passed away. He nodded as I slipped him a sawbuck, the only thing in my wallet. He said not to worry, he'd take care of her. I knew he would. Who wouldn't? I then bid goodbye to Yael and told her everything would be alright. She threw her arms around me, gave me a kiss, and said, "Thank you," before following the bellman inside. With her best runway walk, I watched her incredible derriere disappear into the lobby. She never looked back.

As I drove back to Ari's boat I thought about what Yael must have gone through. I wondered if they were in the middle of it when Ari expired. I told her I'd check up on her, but honestly, I didn't know if I would ever see her again. All I could think of though, as I pictured her naked on the boat, was that she would have no problem getting by in this town. One way or another, women like her never did.

On the way back, I stopped at the little convenience store on Via Marina Way. There was a dumpster out back, and I tossed the trash bag from Ari's boat in there. When I got back to Ari's dock, I grabbed the tool bag out of the way-back and headed for *Above the Line*. Once on the boat, I unlocked the main salon, went in, and locked the door behind me. I climbed down to the master suite and rolled Ari's hairy body over so I could get at the storage compartment underneath the bed. And then it hit me. His bowels and bladder had let loose so the sheets were now foul and soiled and the stench was overwhelming. He'd shit the bed. I remember an old girlfriend back east who used to use that expression for something that conked out. Like, "You're going to have to drive because my car shit the bed," or "My computer crashed and totally shit the bed." I finally found out where that expression came from.

Ari was still weighing the mattress down, making it too heavy to lift so I dragged him over to the far edge of the bed, wedged against the bulkhead. I tried not to breath as I lifted the mattress and opened the storage compartment. The open door to the storage compartment held the mattress up at a roughly forty-five-degree angle, keeping Ari at the low end against the wall.

There it was. Stacks of hundred-dollar bills, bank-banded together in five thousand dollar increments. And there were a lot of them. I opened my tool bag and started to load them in, trying to neatly arrange the stacks into piles. I lost count when I suddenly realized it might not all fit. Thankfully, it did, and I closed the bag tightly with the leather belt straps. I placed the bag on the steps leading up to the main salon and turned back to close the storage compartment and let the mattress down. Ari now lay in a pile of shit-soiled sheets, so I threw the comforter over him.

I went into the head to wash my hands. Lucky thing I did, since I found one of those eyelash curler-clamp things on the sink. I shoved it in my pocket and checked around the master suite one last time for anything else Yael might have left behind.

I was about to gag from the stench, so I headed up to the salon with the tool bag. Again, I checked around inside and scanned the surroundings outside before heading out with the tool bag. I went to the neighbor's boat, climbed in the stern and dropped the bag in my inflatable. I then took out the eyelash curler from my pocket and tossed it in the water. It sank like a stone. I pulled out my phone and dialed 911.

"Hello? I'd like to report a death."

CHAPTER 16

I waited around for the paramedics to show up and, just as I thought, they pronounced Ari dead. I hoped that they would make even more of a mess of things before any police arrived to sort things out, question me, and take statements. I told the paramedics who he was and that I came to check on his boat and found him like this. I tried to administer CPR but it was already too late. They expressed sort of a reserved, quiet, respectful understanding. Or, maybe they just didn't give a crap. It was just another "shitter" to them. Another dead body discovered by a friend or employee, too late, nothing they could do.

The law showed up a little while later. Luckily it was L.A. County deputy sheriffs. They surveyed the scene and came out on the dock to take my statement. They seemed satisfied and didn't deem *Above the Line* a crime scene. They concurred with the paramedics that it looked like natural causes to them. That was until SMPD detectives Gomez and Lo showed up. They spoke to the deputies out of my earshot. The deputies looked back at me and shrugged, seemingly satisfied with what I'd told them, but they now hung back, watching as Gomez and Lo came my way.

"How come whereever you go, Millek, there's a dead body?" Lo asked in his usual accusatory manner.

"You don't think I had anything to do with this, do you?" I asked, knowing full well he did.

"I think you probably had everything to do with it," he said.

"Hey, this just cost me another paycheck. Why would I want to kill him?"

"How much did Goldman owe you?" he asked accusingly.

"Nothing," I told him.

"What? You work on his boat because you're such a nice guy?"

"No, he paid me in advance," I told him. "Should I call my lawyer now, and save you the paperwork, or wait until you press false charges again?"

"No one's pressing charges here, Millek. But why don't you tell us what happened." It was Gomez this time.

I kept to my story that I maintain Ari's boat when he's out of the country. I came to check on things and discovered his body. He was dead when I arrived. I tried CPR, but it was too late.

"Well, we're going to take a look around. We'd appreciate it if you stick around in case we have any further questions," said Gomez.

I was in no mood to be cordial with these assholes. I told them that they had my number and could call me if they had any more questions.

"That your car over there?" Lo pointed. "The Suburban?"

"Yeah, so?"

"Mind if we take a look inside?"

"Only if you tell me what you're looking for," I told him.

"You know what we're looking for, Millek. The money. The money from the Pays Lee murder," he said.

"And you think I have it, and I'm keeping it in my Suburban? Really?" I laughed.

Lo and Gomez exchanged looks.

"Sure, you want to take a look? Come on, I'm going that way anyway," I said and led them off to the Suburban.

I made a big deal out of throwing open all the doors and letting them search the car. The detectives took a perfunctory look around, but when all they saw was my wetsuit, they gave up.

"Don't go far, Millek. We may want to talk to you," Gomez instructed.

"You know where I live. I'll be there," I told them as I got in the Suburban and drove off.

I felt a bit nervous about leaving the tool bag full of money in my inflatable, tied up to the neighbor's boat. But I also felt a pang of pleasure knowing the money was right there under their noses as they canvased the area.

I drove back over to Tiki Marina and parked in the garage. I didn't see Swanzy or the Mustang, and somehow didn't think I would. I went up to my apartment and laid down on the couch, wondering how long I would have to wait for Lo and Gomez to come knocking. I was pretty much expecting it, hoping it would be sooner rather than later, so I could go collect my tool bag. I opened my laptop and checked my email and looked for any news about Ari's death on the internet. Nothing yet, but I knew it wouldn't be long. I thought of calling TMZ and tipping them off, but then thought better of it. Those guys were scum. I might be below the line, but I still had some scruples.

About an hour later, there came a knock on my apartment door. Gomez and Lo, just as I expected. When they asked if they could come in, I was reluctant but wanted to get them out of there as soon as possible, so I let them in.

"We came by to let you know we're ruling Goldman's death as natural causes," said Lo.

"Good job, Sherlock. You come up with that all by yourself?" I asked with as much sarcasm as I could muster.

"No need to be an asshole about it," said Gomez. "You can understand our position, can't you?"

"What I don't understand is why you guys keep hassling me when the guy that killed Pays Lee—*and* my friend Rudy—is still out there somewhere."

"We're working on that. Ever hear of a guy named Ernesto Swanzy?" asked Gomez. I guess it was Gomez's turn to ask the questions. Lo watched me closely, giving me the evil eye the whole time.

I thought about Morris Bigsby's veiled threat, but I didn't bring up Swanzy, Gomez did. No matter, I played dumb.

"Who?"

"Ernesto Swanzy."

"I don't think so, should I have?"

"He was all over the news a few years back," said Lo.

I shrugged.

"You never had any dealings with him?" Gomez asked.

"Not that I know of. Who is he?"

"He's a person of interest. Somebody we've been trying to find."

'Well, he ain't here. Maybe you should be looking somewhere else."

"We are, but if you happen to run across him, we'd appreciate it if you gave us a call," said Gomez.

"And how will I know if I run across him? I don't even know what this guy looks like."

Gomez pulled out a copy of his mug shot, apparently from when he got busted for supplying Michelle Bartley with crack cocaine. The mug shot had to be over ten years old, and Swanzy had a full head of hair, was clean-shaven, and looked about thirty pounds heavier. I stared at it without showing any signs of recognition—signs I knew they were watching me for—then handed it back.

"Sure," was all I said.

"Sure, what?" Lo snapped.

"Sure, if I see this guy, you guys will be the first to know. Okay?" I said.

"We appreciate it," said Gomez. He tapped his partner on the shoulder and nodded toward the door.

"We'll be talking, Millek," said Lo, as if he had the case all tied up to me.

"Yeah, I look forward to it. Next time I'll make tea," I said, again being as sarcastic as I could.

With that, Lo and Gomez were gone. From my balcony, I watched them exit the building and get in their car when the doorbell buzzed. I hit the intercom and heard Molly's voice, I buzzed her in, surprised to hear from her this early in the afternoon. She couldn't have possibly wrapped so soon.

I was at the door waiting by time she got to my door. As soon as she entered, we wrapped our arms around each other and kissed.

"You're early," I said, stating the obvious.

"I quit," she said.

"What?"

"I heard Jimmy fired you, so I made a couple of phone calls and found someone to replace me. Jane was totally cool about it. Disappointed, but cool."

"That's crazy," I told Molly. "You shouldn't have quit because of me."

"It wasn't because of you. It was because of Jimmy," she said. "I was not going to put up with his crap for another twelve weeks. He was spying on me. Telling me how to run my life. This is why we're getting a divorce. It was stupid of me to think we could work together on this film."

"What about the money? I mean, do you have another gig?" I asked.

"No. I think I need some time away. Some time off. I've got enough to last until house gets sold, so I'm not too concerned about the money."

The mention of money made me think of the tool bag full of cash sitting in my inflatable.

"Look, Molly, I'm glad you're here but I wasn't expecting you until later..."

"I'm sorry, I should have called. I was so wound up..."

"No, no, it's okay. I got to run over to the next basin and get my dinghy. I left it over at a client's boat. He passed away this morning."

"What? Oh my god!"

"Yeah. Ari Goldman, remember him?"

"The producer? God, I worked for him years ago when I was first starting out."

I reminded her that we both worked on the low-budget ninja movie Ari produced years ago, and we shared a laugh.

"*Renegade Blade!*"

"Right!" I laughed.

We embraced again before I left. I told her I'd be back shortly and that I'd take her out to a nice dinner. She kissed me deeply and whispered in my ear, "Let's have something delivered."

I told her okay and felt a quiver in my jeans. Molly seemed to have that effect on me. I kissed her again and told her I'd be right back.

I walked as briskly as I could back to C Basin without breaking into a run and causing suspicion. I scanned the area and all seemed calm. There were still a couple of forensic officers in deputy sheriff windbreakers hanging around, taking measurements and writing notes. I didn't see any of the officers from earlier, and no Gomez or Lo. I guessed that they'd already removed Ari's body, and the forensics were doing wrap-up work. As I strolled down the dock, neither of them batted an eye at me.

I climbed aboard the neighbor's sailboat and down into my dinghy. The tool bag was still there and looked untouched. I opened it just enough to see the money was still there. As usual, I rowed out to about halfway down the basin before I pulled the engine cord and puttered my way back to B Basin.

When I got to *Stella,* I killed the engine and tossed the tool bag into the cockpit before climbing aboard myself. I went below and transferred the money into the Pelican case. I made sure the case was closed snugly and sealed it with a couple of cable ties in the lock holes. I tied the half-inch braided line to the handle and the short piece to the Danforth anchor. The sun was beginning to set, and I squinted as I took my rig up on deck and walked up to the bow. I lowered the anchor into the water, followed by the Pelican case. I held on to the bitter end of the rope and watched them sink. When they hit the bottom, I dragged the line so the anchor would set then ran the line back through a snap shackle, around a winch in the cockpit, finally securing it to a cleat. I walked up to the bow again to check and all I could see was the braided anchor line disappearing into the dark, murky marina water. From *Above the Line* to below the line, the water line, I thought smiling to myself.

CHAPTER 17

I headed back to my apartment anticipating another fine evening with Molly. But when I opened the door to my apartment, Molly was standing there, frozen, fear on her face. I walked in, and the door slammed behind me. As I spun around, Swanzy was there, and he cracked the butt of his pistol against my temple. I heard Molly scream as I went down, and Swanzy yelled at her to "Shut up!"

I struggled to my knees, the world spinning, temple pounding. Molly rushed to my side, but Swanzy was there and pulled her away by her hair. I was still trying to put everything together as to what was going on, but seeing Swanzy manhandle Molly made everything clear, and I lunged for him. Unfortunately I was still unsteady, so it was easy for him to sidestep me, pound me on the back, and send me to the floor again. As I struggled to my knees the second time, the kick to my still-sore ribs flipped me over, reeling in pain and seeing stars. I heard Molly scream again then the distinct *thwack* of a slap. I lay there helpless for a moment, trying to focus on my spinning world when Swanzy loomed over me, pointing his gun in my face. All I could do was bring my arms up in a feeble attempt to protect my face from what I was sure going to be my immediate demise. Instead, Swanzy bent over and pulled me up by the front of my shirt.

I looked to Molly as I struggled to my feet. She was holding her face where the dirtbag had smacked her. Swanzy now had his pistol firmly planted under my chin as he turned back to Molly, "One more fucking sound out of you, and I blow your boyfriend's head off. Got it?!"

Molly nodded as she sobbed and looked to me. I tried to reassure her by nodding, but Swanzy dug the pistol harder into the underside of my chin.

"What do you want?" It came out as more of a mumble.

"You know what I want! I want that package you just sank over the side of your boat," he said.

"What are you talking about?"

"We just watched you sink it, asshole!" He said pointing to my balcony window.

I looked to Molly for a reaction, but she simply looked scared and frightened.

"All right, all right. Lets go get it," I said.

"We're *all* going to go get it. And then we're gonna go for a little boat ride."

So this was it. Swanzy was obviously the killer, and I knew once he had the money, he'd want to clean up any loose ends. Molly and me were definitely loose ends.

"Lets go!" he barked and turned to Molly. "You too, freckles."

Swanzy shoved me toward the door and grabbed Molly, pulling her close and sticking the pistol in her ribs.

"We're going to go out to your boat, real quiet-like. Like we're all good friends, got it?" He waited for Molly to nod in agreement before turning back to me. "Be cool, or your old lady gets it," he said, accentuating his point by jabbing her in the ribs with the muzzle of his gun, making her jump.

"Look, leave her out of this, your beef's with me. I'll give you what you want. There's no need to bring her…"

"Shut up! I'm giving the orders here. Now get moving!"

I looked to Molly again and tried to reassure her with my eyes. I could tell I wasn't doing a very good job, not with a pistol pointed in her side. I opened the door and started out. My mind was racing—how was I going to get us out of this predicament? Forget about above the line or below the line, this was the end of the line. I had to figure something out. But it was hard to think. My head was still reeling and my ribs throbbed with each step. Was this really how I was going to die? I was now wishing I'd fessed up about Swanzy to Gomez and Lo and told them everything I knew. I hoped like hell those two still suspected me and were watching me. I looked around hoping I could signal them in some way if they were there, but I didn't see any sign of them. Figured. Of course they weren't around when I finally needed them. And I wasn't armed because of them.

The fresh evening air and the walk cleared my head somewhat as I led the way down to the dock. Swanzy followed holding Molly close, his gun hidden under his jacket but still pressed against her ribs. As we boarded *Stella*, Swanzy shoved Molly onto the cockpit bench.

"Hey, easy!" I snapped at Swanzy. Then to Molly, "Are you okay?"

I got a quick nod from her as Swanzy shoved me toward the companionway.

"Open up," he ordered.

I unlocked the padlock and pulled apart the hatch boards. Once the door was open, he grabbed Molly by the arm and led her below. I was about to follow when he turned and pointed his gun at me.

"No, you get the money."

With his gun he pointed to the line that was tied off to the winch and instructed me to retrieve the Pelican case. I undid the line from the winch and tried to haul it up but the anchor was holding fast. Swanzy saw I was having a hard time, so I asked him to pass up a winch handle and told him they were in a drawer near where he was standing. He found one and tossed it up at me.

"Let's go," he barked impatiently.

I wrapped the line around the winch, inserted the handle and began to crank. Slowly the line came up and eventually the Pelican case broke the surface. I managed a couple more turns of the crank until the case bounced off *Stella*'s hull. I tied off the line and reached over the side to pull it aboard. My ribs were screaming in pain as I struggled to get it aboard, and the weight of the anchor attached made it even more difficult.

"Don't try anything funny, lover-boy, or the bitch gets it," Swanzy called out watching me from inside the cabin.

Lying on my stomach over the side made my aching ribs hurt even more as I dragged the case over the side followed by the anchor. I looked to the companionway past Swanzy to try and get a look at Molly, but he had her seated out of my sightline.

"Bring it here." He motioned with the pistol as I dragged the case and the anchor to the companionway and down into the salon. I was now able to see Molly and it was hard to say whether she was silently scared or silently pissed. I guessed it was both. Swanzy directed me to put the case on the table and start the engine. I did what I was told, and he pulled out a knife and cut the cable ties. As the engine sputtered to life, Swanzy undid the latches and threw open the case revealing the neatly banded, stack bills. Molly saw it and shot me a look. I couldn't look her in the eyes, giving her a rather pathetic nod. I should have come clean with Molly about the money from the start, and now she was in danger because of it.

Swanzy flipped through a couple of the stacks to make sure it was all cash and smiled at the result. Satisfied he looked to me and said, "Okay, captain, let's shove off."

"Look, you got the money," I said. "Just go, leave us..."

"Uh-uh, don't work like that." he said.

"Where we going?" I asked feebly.

"I'll tell you when we get there." He directed me up to the cockpit.

I told him I had to go up to the bow to untie the dock lines, so he took a step up on the companionway to watch, keeping his pistol trained on Molly.

"Don't do anything stupid if you care about your girlfriend's health," he said. I went up to the bow and untied the dock lines cutting *Stella* loose. Back in the cockpit I untied the stern dock lines, got behind the wheel, backed *Stella* out of her slip, and motored down the basin toward the main channel. While Swanzy's attention was focused on Molly below, I unraveled the main sheet. I thought if I could get Swanzy on deck, maybe I could let the main loose, cross the wind, and whack him in the head with the mainsail boom. A relatively easy maneuver if I could only catch him standing in the cockpit. I started thinking of other options for fighting back if the opportunity presented itself.

The sun was setting, the sky darkening, and I neglected to turn on my running lights in hopes that maybe the Coast Guard would notice as I passed their base. They might send out a patrol boat to issue me a citation. I could pass their base dangerously close if Swanzy stayed below. But suddenly the running lights came on, along with the reddened cabin lights below. Swanzy's face appeared in in the companionway and smirked. He had obviously found the switch panel.

"Nice try, asshole."

"What?" I played dumb.

"I know my way around boats, so don't be trying to pull something over on me."

I wondered how well he knew his way around boats. He looked out, scanning the area as we entered the darkened main channel then directed me to turn right toward the breakwater and out to the Pacific.

"Make sure you give that Coast Guard station a wide berth, and don't do anything stupid," he instructed.

As we cleared the south end of the breakwater, he led Molly out into the cockpit and followed, gun trained on us. He sat Molly on the starboard side, and he sat on the port side near the controls and throttled up the engine.

"Want to set sails? I'm not sure how much fuel I've got," I asked.

"Just keep motoring, nice and smooth. I don't want to do any heeling," he said.

He told me to head due south, a beeline toward Catalina Island. I wondered what he had in mind so I asked him.

"Catalina?"

"To provision. Then Mexico."

"I didn't bring my passport."

"You won't need it," he laughed.

"So is that your plan? Deep six our bodies and head to Mexico? You can probably buy a new life down there with all that money, I guess." I tested the waters.

"Something like that," he replied.

Molly and I exchanged a look.

"So why'd you do it?" I asked.

"Do what?"

"Kill Pays Lee? His crew? Kill Rudy?"

"Pays Lee had it coming. He had it coming for a long time."

"No doubt," I said, egging him on.

"Pays Lee was the one that destroyed Michelle, but they all blamed me!"

"Michelle Bartley?"

He nodded. "Yeah, she was no angel, but we were in love. I was her bodyguard, you know. But I was more than that. We spent a lot of time together, on the road and off. And then that motherfucker Pays Lee came into the picture and took advantage of her. Got her hooked on the shit."

Swanzy went on about how he and Michelle had an ongoing affair while she was on the concert circuit. How she would call him up to her room whenever she was feeling lonely. That Michelle Bartley's whole downfall coincided with Pays Lee producing her Bessie Wallace tribute album. How Pays turned her on to crack cocaine and heroin in order to get that bluesy sound. How Michelle continued using when she then got the role to play Bessie Wallace in the biopic. How Pays got her hooked then used her habit to take advantage of her sexually.

When Pays tossed her aside, it was Swanzy who Michelle depended on to supply her. Swanzy said he was in love with her and just wanted to make her happy.

"I tried to get her clean and make her stop. But she had power over me. And, she used it if I didn't do what she wanted."

While Swanzy opened up, I kept looking over at Molly who sat there quietly taking it all in. She did give me a nod of encouragement at one point, and I took it to mean to keep Swanzy talking.

Then he dropped the bombshell, "You know he's the father of her daughter?"

"What?"

"Yeah," he said.

"Who? Lauren?" I asked.

Swanzy nodded.

My jaw dropped. Those pictures. The video. The back of my Suburban. Realizing that he had been taking advantage of his own daughter made me even more disgusted.

"Slime bag!" I blurted it out involuntarily.

Molly sat quietly, wide-eyed taking it all in.

"No fucking shit!" replied an emotionally-charged Swanzy.

"Wait, did Pays Lee know that? That he was Michelle's father?"

"Of course he fucking knew! He knew. Michelle knew. And I knew. And of course Pichter found out, eventually. He's the one that bailed me out and buried the story that I was Michelle's supplier once he got involved with her. He wanted to hush everything up. And he paid me to keep quiet."

"He pay you to kill Pays Lee?" I asked.

"That was Michelle's idea. She's the one that called me on it. I don't know why, but something must have happened recently to piss her off. But you know what? I was happy to do it. I wanted to kill that bastard for years. Michelle didn't have to ask twice. Only *you* ended up with my money!"

His anger was suddenly directed back at me, so I tried to

steer it away, and press him for more info.

"Hey, I didn't know! Pays Lee owed me a bunch of money, and I took what I thought was mine."

"He didn't owe you that much!"

Molly looked back and forth between Swanzy and me.

"I wasn't going to hang around and count it. I just grabbed it and ran. Why didn't you take it?"

"Because that other guy in the Charger showed up. And then you!" Swanzy said.

"Rudy," I said. Molly and I shared a look.

Swanzy went on to recap his version of what happened that night at the airport, how Michelle made all the arrangements. He had already received fifty thousand dollars as a down payment, and Pays Lee would be holding the rest so it would look like a rip-off. Only Rudy showed up at exactly the wrong time. Swanzy emerged from the shadows and shot Rudy in the head. Then he shot Omar. Swanzy said he smiled as Pays Lee begged for his life then shot him point blank in the head. He shot him again in the chest when he was down. He was about to go for the money but saw headlights approaching. My headlights. He panicked, went for the Rudy's Charger, shoved the body over and sped out, passing me on my way in. He parked in the nearby industrial park and waited for me to leave. When I did, he went after me.

"How did you know I had the money?" I asked.

"Why else would you be leaving so soon? Anyone else would have called the cops and waited. But you left. And you left fast. A sure sign you had it," he said. He was right. I couldn't argue with that.

Even though I'd lost Swanzy in the chase that night, he tracked me down through my license plate number. I briefly wondered if he had called Morris Bigsby to get the plate info on me as I did on him. He ditched the Charger with Rudy's body in it a few miles away from the crime scene up on Temescal Canyon, near the trailer park where he lived.

I thought of what might have happened if I had arrived on time that night. Sure, I might be dead too, but maybe I could have prevented Swanzy from killing Rudy, and Pays Lee for that matter. It didn't matter much now. If I didn't think of something soon, both Molly and me would be Swanzy's next victims.

Swanzy stayed seated the whole time so trying to back-wind the boom was not going to work unless I could get him to stand up. Molly was still watching me, as if she were waiting for me to get us out of this mess. I noticed her shiver and got an idea.

"Ernesto, there's some sweatshirts and fleeces down below. I think the lady's a bit chilly," I said.

"You won't be needing them," was all he said as he scanned the area around us.

We were about an hour outside the breakwater motoring at about five knots so we were pretty much in the middle of the bay. There wasn't another boat or ship in sight, and the crescent moon did little to illuminate our surroundings or make us visible to anyone on shore. I knew I had to come up with something, and it had to be soon. Swanzy was sitting just out of reach, gun pointed in our general direction. Behind him, still in the winch was the winch handle I used to retrieve the Pelican case. I tried to gauge if I could somehow grab it and use it to whack him. It was a long shot and he'd have to be distracted somehow.

I waited until Swanzy checked our surroundings again, this time up ahead. I looked to Molly and gave her a nod. I couldn't tell what was actually on her mind but she seemed to understand and looked ready to act on my cue. When Swanzy looked forward, I reached over, floored the throttle and cut the wheel. The force threw him back, and I lunged for him, grabbing his gun hand and wrestling him down onto the cockpit bench. I had his gun arm pinned as we rolled off the bench onto the deck floor. He squeezed off a shot that went wild.

"The winch handle!" I shouted to Molly.

She climbed around the wheel to go for it, and luckily cut the wheel in the other direction, slamming Swanzy's back into the bench. Molly stopped short of the winch handle when she saw Swanzy's gun hand swing around with me still holding on. He squeezed off another shot up in the air near Molly. Swanzy and I wrestled for control of the gun, me trying to get him to drop it and him trying to point it at me, his finger still on the trigger. We struggled to our knees and as we were getting to our feet, Molly came down hard with the winch handle. But the boat bounced and she missed his head, landing a weak blow to his shoulder. I saw the sail boom come swinging and ducked in time as it cracked Swanzy in the head. That was enough for him to drop the gun. I shoved him away and dove for the gun as it slid across the deck to the stern corner of the cockpit. I was about to grab it but Swanzy jumped on my back, threw an arm around my neck pulling me away in a chokehold. I tried twisting out of his hold and elbowing him but to no avail. He had me from behind in a neck lock. The more I struggled to reach the gun, the tighter his hold on my neck, and the weaker I got. The boat was bouncing, going round in circles, and every time I reached for it, the gun slid further away from my grasp. Gasping for air, my vision was going and I felt myself blacking-out.

Suddenly a shot rang out and I heard Swanzy shout. My ears were ringing, and Swanzy still managed to keep a tight hold on my neck even as I tried in vain to pry myself out of his grip. Then, another shot. Finally his hold loosened, his body went limp, and I felt him roll off me to the deck. Struggling to catch my breath I looked behind me and saw Molly, pistol in hand. She had come up beside us, grabbed the gun and fired point blank into Swanzy's ribs. He now lay in the cockpit, either dead or dying, bleeding out from his wounds.

I turned and killed the throttle. The engine puttered out and stalled. I struggled to my feet and turned to Molly who stood there, shocked, gun still in hand looking down at man she just killed. Still panting, I gently reached over and took the gun out of her hand, and put it in the winch handle pocket at the helm. She looked up at me, tears in her eyes, and threw her arms around me, sobbing.

"It's okay, it's okay," I managed to get out while holding her tight, trying to reassure her.

"Is he...?" she asked through her sobs.

"I think so," I said as I looked down at Swanzy. His eyes were frozen open in a death stare.

"I didn't mean to..."

"Hey, you saved our lives! It was either him or us."

I held Molly tightly, trying to comfort her as she heaved in sobs, burying her face into my chest.

"Are you okay? Did he hurt you?" I asked.

"Yes. I mean no. I mean, I'm okay. He didn't..."

Finally, she looked down at Swanzy and then up at me, wiping her eyes.

"What are we going to do?"

Exactly what I was thinking.

"We have to call the police," she said frantically, pushing me away.

"Hang on. Calm down," I said trying to buy time to think. I pulled her close again and held her tight.

Calling the police was not the first thing I thought of doing. I was thinking more about how to avoid calling them. I'd have to somehow hide the money first if we were to turn back and call them. And to do that with Swanzy's body aboard? It would be too difficult to explain. I also had to get Molly's take on the money, because she was now my partner in all this.

As she began to calm down, and I finally caught my breath I said, "Well, I guess we can go back and report this whole thing to the police but it probably won't fare well with me, on account of the money. And on account a lot of people winding up dead because of it."

"You had the money all along, didn't you?" she said in anger and pounded my chest.

"Yes. Yes, I did. But I couldn't tell you! I didn't want to put you in danger."

169

"Didn't want to put me in danger?! What do you call all this?"

"I know, I know. I'm sorry I wasn't honest with you. I thought the less you knew about the money, the better off you'd be. I mean if the police questioned you."

"You bastard!"

"I'm sorry, Molly. Please don't..."

"How much is there?" she asked.

"Over eight hundred thousand."

"What are you going to do with it?"

"I was going to send half to Rudy's sister. The rest...?"

Molly shook her head, "We have to go to the police."

"If that's what you want, okay. But that probably means me going to jail."

Molly took a moment and thought about that. Then she said, "What about me? Will I get arrested for killing him?"

"No! No, it was self-defense. I'll tell them it was me."

"No, we can't lie. They'll figure it out."

"It may be hard to prove."

She thought about it some more. "Who would get the money if we went to the police?"

"That's a good question. We'd have to tell them everything. All about Michelle Bartley and her affairs with Pays Lee and Swanzy. About Lauren being Pays Lee's daughter and what I saw on her phone. And about Pichter, him no doubt having a hand in all this. Of course, they'll never believe me. Pichter wouldn't let them. He's too powerful. Might even be suicide. Who knows what he'd do. Even if I..." I stopped.

"Even if you what?"

I sighed and said, "I made copies of the pictures and video on Lauren's phone. For insurance, so to speak. But even if I showed them to the police, it wouldn't prove anything about Pichter."

"It would give him the motive. Isn't that what police are always looking for? Motive?"

"All he has to do is deny ever seeing them. If he hasn't seen the photos or the video, he has no motive. And then the question would come—what I was doing with them? They'd probably throw a child pornography possession charge at me to boot."

We both stood there thinking everything over as the boat bobbed up and down drifting aimlessly in the middle of the bay.

"As far as the money goes, I guess technically it was Pays Lee's, but I imagine it would be tied up as evidence for a couple of years. We'd never see it again, that's for sure. And Rudy's sister wouldn't get a dime."

"The fact that Pichter was able to give you his name means he was tied into this in some way," she said pointing to Swanzy's body. "We can tell that to the police."

"Again, he can simply deny it. Or he can just say he recognized the picture I texted Bigsby. Ernesto did work for Michelle Bartley in the past and made some headlines. No reason Pichter wouldn't know who he is if he saw his picture."

We both pondered in silence, staring at Ernesto Swanzy on the cockpit floor.

Then with a determined coldness suddenly in her tone, "Can we dump his body overboard?" she asked, snapping her gaze from Swanzy to me.

I looked her in the eyes, gauging her seriousness. I was happy that she had been the one to make that suggestion, because it was exactly what I had been thinking.

"Yes...yes, we can. But we've got to do it right. So he won't ever come back to haunt us."

CHAPTER 18

I figured that to get rid of Swanzy's body right, we needed to anchor the body to the bottom of the bay. Decaying bodies always produce gas in the organs and intestines, and eventually float to the surface. If we could anchor him to the bottom, the body wouldn't float to the surface, and the fish would clean up the rest. No body, no evidence. As far as anyone would know, Swanzy would have just up and disappeared along with the money.

I had *Stella's* twenty-five pound plow anchor, chain, and a long length of rope to set it. I took Molly's hand as we climbed over Swanzy's body, careful not to walk through the puddle of blood, and we went below to consult the local nautical chart. We were sitting in waters that were about six hundred feet deep. Too deep. If we headed back directly toward the coast, we could cut that depth in half. I had a spool of rope long enough to tie it to the forty feet of anchor chain and two hundred feet of rope I already had so we could set the anchor on the bottom and then toss the line overboard. By doing so, Swanzy's body would be anchored to the bottom of three hundred feet of water with no visual cue leading to the surface. It would be better than giving him "concrete galoshes." I filled Molly in on the plan and brought out the warmest fleece jacket I could find for her. Back up on deck, I started the engine and headed back toward the mainland. I asked Molly to take the helm, giving her a bearing back toward the coast. I threw a blanket over Swanzy so Molly wouldn't have to look at him as I went below to gather the things I needed for the anchor rig.

Twenty minutes later, decked out in my foul weather overall pants and rubber boots, I manhandled the anchor and forty feet of chain into the cockpit. Checking the depth gauge, I saw we were headed in the right area. When it read two-eighty, I had Molly put the engine in neutral and hit the kill switch. My plan was to use the hundred feet of spooled line I had stowed in the cockpit lazarette that I got as partial payment on a rigging job. I went about adding it to my anchor rode of forty feet of chain and two hundred feet of rope.

Next came the gruesome work of securing Swanzy's body to the end of the chain. I told Molly to keep a look-out in case any other boats approached the area, and I went to work. Kneeling over his body in the blood puddle, I wrapped the chain around Swanzy's limbs and secured it using plastic cable ties. I wrapped Swanzy's wrists and ankles to the chain using cable ties too. He was now strung up to the end of the chain with his hands over his head, the chain wrapped around his torso, and ankles tied to the chain. I then tied the line to the end of the anchor chain and unrolled it to get to the other end. That meant unspooling the entire length of the line in the tight cockpit, and keeping it untangled, no small feat. The more I worked, the more my hands and overalls got covered in Swanzy's blood. Molly stood at the stern rail and watched with a sort of stoic morbid fascination that made me a little uneasy. I told her again to make sure she to keep an eye out for other boats.

Once I was finished, I started to play out the anchor and chain over the side, letting it sink. When the chain came toward the end, I struggled with the grisly task of lifting Swanzy's body up to the side. I stopped when the body was hanging over the side, held by the anchor line secured to a winch. I'd heard that body gases formed mostly in the stomach, and I wanted to make sure that Swanzy stayed on the bottom. So I told Molly to look away as I pulled out my dive knife. I held my breath and stabbed Swanzy's stomach, tearing it open, gutting him like a fish. Blood and guts spilled into the water, leaving a long line of bloody intestines trailing out of the cavity. I gave his body one last shove over the side, and with a splash he sunk like a rock, dragged down by the anchor and chain. I let the anchor line out, and it ran down fast, pulled by all the weight. The line in the cockpit disappeared as it ran over the side. I looked down at my bloody hands and suddenly felt sick. I leaned over the side and puked my guts up as the line continued to run out from the cockpit. I was dry heaving when I suddenly panicked there wouldn't be enough line. I grabbed the bitter end and quickly tied it off to a cleat so as not to lose it overboard. Finally, the line went slack when the anchor hit bottom. There was only about ten feet of the line still on board.

Wiping my mouth and spitting the foul taste out of my mouth, I took off my bloodied jacket and tossed it overboard. Molly watched as I started the engine and threw it in reverse pulling backward until the line went taut setting the anchor. Once I was satisfied that it was properly set, I freed the line from the cleat and tied the bitter end to the Danforth anchor I bought the day before. Tossing it overboard I watched it sink, taking the end of the line and any trace of Ernesto Swanzy with it into the deep. Molly came up behind me, wrapped her arms around me and laid her head on my back sobbing.

I looked down at the bloody mess in the cockpit. "You have to be anywhere in the morning?" I asked.

I felt her head shake and her voice cracked as she said, "No."

"Good. Let's go to Catalina."

I turned *Stella* around and headed on a dead reckoning for Avalon. I put a teary-eyed Molly in charge of the helm and gave her a compass heading hoping that having something to do would shake her despair. I then started to pull up buckets of seawater from over the side, and scrub out the cockpit. I soaped, bleached, and rinsed numerous times until the water ran clean out of the scuppers. I wanted to be certain there were no traces of Swanzy's blood left behind. I picked up Swanzy's pistol and was about to throw it over the side when it occurred to me it might come in handy. It was a .40 caliber Smith & Wesson, and I thought it was safe to assume it was the weapon used to kill Pays Lee, Rudy, and Omar. I placed it back in the winch handle pocket to keep it nearby, but also in case I needed to throw it over the side in a hurry.

Convinced things were cleaned up, I pulled off my boots and foul weather overall pants and tossed them overboard. With Molly still at the helm, I shook out the mainsail and unfurled the jib. We had a nice westerly breeze that held us on a beam reach. We were able to kill the engine and sail. I checked on Molly, and it was like she was already trying to put the events of the evening behind her. Other than her swollen reddened eyes, at the wheel with the wind in her hair, steering *Stella* in the dim moonlight, she looked liked a vision. A vision of beauty. A vision of strength. She looked in her element. If I wasn't in love with her already, I was now.

"You okay?" I asked.

She nodded and managed a smile, apparently enjoying the task of steering on the ocean swells. I watched her for another moment committing the vision to memory before I went below and put on some dry warm clothes and a pot of coffee. Waiting for the kettle to boil, I suddenly felt drained and dead tired but still kept asking myself- Had I done everything to get rid of all signs of Swanzy being aboard? Could we really get away with all this, and the money? Would Molly be able to keep our secret? All I wanted to do was go to sleep and turn my mind off. But I knew it would still be a while before I would be able to get some rest.

When the coffee was done I returned to the cockpit with a mug for Molly. She looked tired but somewhat content. There was something new and different about her. I saw a quiet resolute strength. She was the perfect picture of a steadfast sailing woman. I could not believe how quickly she seemingly bounced back from everything that we'd been through that night. But, because of her I felt as if suddenly a great weight had been lifted off me, and for the first time in days felt as though I could actually relax.

We greeted the rising sun with another pot of coffee, and Santa Catalina Island came into view as we cruised along its coast toward Avalon. We'd only had one close run-in with a freighter in the shipping channel while it was still dark, with Molly still at the helm. I instructed her to aim for his stern, and I set the sails accordingly. We never got closer than two miles, but at night on the water those huge container ships will raise the hairs on the back of your neck. There's no way they're going to get out of your way whether you have the right of way or not. Cross them, and they'll run you down without even knowing they did. Molly handled it like a pro, with more curiosity than fear.

We got to Avalon Bay around 7:00 a.m. I had taken over the helm a couple of hours earlier while Molly slept on the cockpit bench, curled up in my sleeping bag. As we approached the harbor, I started the engine, furled the jib, and lowered the main. My climbing around the cockpit woke Molly, and she peered around in the bright morning sunlight, sleepy-eyed, remembering where she was.

"Are we there yet?" she asked.

"Aye, matey," I replied.

I pulled up and moored to Doug Strong's mooring. I had an open invitation to use his mooring there if I ever needed it, as long as he wasn't using it or hadn't loaned it to someone else. Luckily, it was vacant, and before long, we were moored. Exhaustion hit me as soon as I was done securing *Stella*. I went down below and climbed into the fore bunk without even bothering to undress. I felt Molly crawl in next to me and snuggle up, but I was asleep before she settled in.

CHAPTER 19

I awoke in the early afternoon to find Molly leaning on her elbows looking straight at me. It startled me, and a flood of memories from the night before flashed before me.

"What?!" I asked, sitting up in a panic.

"Nothing. I was just watching you sleep," she said.

"God, you scared the shit out of me."

"I'm sorry," she laughed.

"Very funny," I mumbled, trying to drive the cobwebs from my brain.

Molly crawled over and gave me a kiss. I put my arms around her and pulled her close. I held her tightly and she laid her head on my chest. I smelled the sweet salt scent in her hair and all was right in my universe.

"You know you have nothing to eat on this boat," she stated.

"I take it you're hungry?"

"Aren't you?"

"Starving," I said, suddenly feeling it. I couldn't remember the last time I ate.

"So what are we going to do about it?"

"We're going to go to the best restaurant in town."

We took quick showers and changed into some extra clothes I had aboard. I put on a varnished-stained sweatshirt and Molly an old cable knit sweater that was way too big for her. She tied her hair back in a ponytail, and she looked great. Molly was like that. She could dress in rags, and she'd still look like she just walked off the cover of a magazine. When we were ready, I took a few hundreds from the Pelican case, got on the radio, and called the water taxi to pick us up since my inflatable was still tied up to my dock back in Marina Del Rey. Before leaving, I stashed the Pelican case in one of the clothes lockers and locked up the boat when we left.

When we hit town, we walked into the first place we saw that looked good and ordered margaritas and ceviche while we perused the rest of the menu. We had a window seat overlooking the harbor, and I could see *Stella* from where we sat. That made me feel a little better since I wasn't too comfortable leaving all that cash aboard unattended. The margarita was going right to my head, and I was starting to unwind. I was able to focus on Molly and purely enjoy being with her. The mood really lightened with the second margarita and something in our bellies. We spoke softly of how we found ourselves together in this place, of what transpired the night before. We reached across the table and took each other's hands. Silently, we stared into each other's eyes, so much being said without a word spoken. The spell broke when our main course of lobster enchiladas and fish tacos arrived.

After dinner, coffee, and sharing a decadent concoction of a dessert they called Buffalo Pie, we went out for a walk around town. We had decided to spend at least a couple of days here, lay low, and monitor the news in case anything came up. Strolling around Avalon we stopped at a few shops to buy some new clothes. Forever the wardrobe mistress, Molly picked out a couple of Hawaiian shirts and a pair of linen pants for me, and few islandy items for herself. We also hit the Von's supermarket for some food and drinks to bring back aboard *Stella*. We were walking back to the water taxi pier when we decided to stop for drink before calling it a day. We chose an upscale restaurant and took a seat at the crowded bar, stuffing our shopping bags underneath. As our margaritas arrived, I looked around the restaurant. There across the room, seated by herself at a table in a dark corner was none other than Michelle Bartley.

"Holy shit!" I muttered, as I turned my back to her, my heart suddenly pounding.

Michelle Bartley had aged well since her days in the spotlight and despite her drug days. She almost looked exactly the same as she did in her heyday. She still had that thin shapely body, long dark curly hair, and stunning good looks that made her an international star. She sat by herself, reading and typing something on her smart phone.

"What?" Molly asked and followed my gaze. "Michelle Bartley! What's she doing here?"

I didn't have an answer but said, "Come on, let's go," and stood up, but immediately froze when the front door opened and in walked Carl complete with his khaki pants and sport jacket.

"Wait." I sat back down and turned away hoping he wouldn't see me.

"What?" asked a confused Molly as she sat back down.

As I observed Carl in the mirror behind the bar, my ribs began to ache. I watched as he casually scanned the room, teeming with diners waiting and cocktail hour revelers. He gave us no notice, and zeroed in on Michelle. He went straight over to her table.

I had my back to them but kept peeking over while I tried to figure out why they were here. I suddenly felt very vulnerable about *Stella* sitting out at the mooring unoccupied with all that cash aboard.

"Why do you think she's here?" Molly whispered.

"I don't know, but I don't like it."

"Do you know that guy she's with?"

"Yeah, that's Carl. The guy I told you about who black-and-blued my ribs," I said.

"The bodyguard?"

"Shhh. Uh-huh" I nodded as Molly took a look over her shoulder at them.

"She must really have a thing for bodyguards. They look

kind of cozy with each other," she whispered.

I glanced back and saw Michelle Bartley reach across the table to take Carl's hand. Carl had his head down and it appeared that Michelle was trying to cheer him up. Was Jonathan Pichter around too? I half-expected to see him walk through the door. He didn't, and when Michelle and Carl became engaged in conversation, I threw down a couple of twenties and gathered up our bags.

"Come on, let's get out of here," I told Molly and I grabbed her arm, leading her out the door.

We hustled over to the water taxi dock. I kept a look out to see if either of them followed or if Pichter was around while we waited for our ride back to *Stella*. I started to panic. Could Carl have found *Stella* while Molly and me were strolling the streets of Avalon and doing our shopping?

"You think this could just be a coincidence?" Molly asked.

"I wish I knew. Somehow, I doubt it."

"Why don't we wait and follow them?"

"I want to check on *Stella* first. Make sure she hasn't been broken into it," I said, trying to sound the least bit paranoid as I could muster.

As the water taxi approached, Molly came up with an idea. "Wait. Why don't I go back and keep an eye on them while you go check on the boat. They won't recognize me so they won't be suspicious. I can try and get a table nearby. Maybe pick up some of their conversation."

"Too dangerous. You don't know this guy Carl."

"And he doesn't know me. Which means he won't even notice me."

She had a point. "What about Michelle? You worked on the Bessie flick. Will she remember you?" I asked.

"I doubt it. That was what, twelve years ago? And if she does, I'll simply play dumb and be gracious."

I thought about it for a moment. "You have your phone?"

Molly pulled it out to show me.

"Okay. Stay in touch. I'll text you when I'm on my way back." Molly leaned over and kissed me before getting up to go. I grabbed her arm and turned her around to face me. "Be careful! Okay?"

She smiled, leaned in, and gave me another kiss. "I will. Don't worry," she said.

Molly strolled off back toward the restaurant as I gathered up the shopping bags and hopped aboard the docking water taxi.

I was relieved to find *Stella* as I'd left her. Locked up tight and seemingly unmolested. I told the water taxi to pick me up on the way back after shuttling a couple of other passengers to their high-end motor yachts. Down in the cabin, I put the bags down and checked on the Pelican case. Everything appeared to be as it should be. I locked *Stella* back up and waited for the water taxi for a ride back to shore. As the water taxi returned to pick me up, I received a text message from Molly. Except it wasn't a text at all. It was a photo of Carl and Michelle. Molly was obviously sitting at a table nearby, and they were now sitting closer, *much* closer, leaning into each other, holding hands, and looking way cozier than before. There was definitely something going on there, and if not, it sure looked like it.

I texted Molly back and asked if she'd overheard any of what they were saying. She wrote back that she'd picked up bits and pieces, but it sounded like they were waiting for someone. I figured it could have only been one of two people, Jonathan Pichter or Ernesto Swanzy. Judging from the photo Molly texted me, it probably wasn't Jonathan Pichter. Had Michelle played Swanzy, promising him some kind of runaway rendezvous, knowing how infatuated he was with her? But now it looked like she had designs on Carl. Could she be using him for the muscle to get the money and/or silence Swanzy? It all made me wonder what made Michelle Bartley tick. Was she back to being a user? Was she out to protect her daughter? Or was she a ruthless manipulator? First Swanzy, back when she was still a superstar singing diva. Then Pichter, who saved her from almost certain ruin, maybe even death. And now Carl? What kind of designs did she have on him? Or was she just getting back at the world for what Pays Lee had done to her?

Staring at the picture of Michelle and Carl that Molly sent, I decided to take a chance. I forwarded it to Morris Bigsby with the message, *Thought your client may want to see this,* and left it like that. I texted Molly to let me know if either Michelle or Carl got a phone call. By time the water taxi dropped me off at the dock, the sun was setting and my phone was ringing. It was Bigsby.

"Hello, Mister Bigsby? How are you?" I said as I answered the call.

"Good evening, Mister Millek. My client is very interested to find out when and where that photo you sent was taken," he asked, getting right to the point.

"It's a very nice restaurant called Casa del Mar in Avalon on Santa Catalina Island. I haven't actually eaten there yet but I hear the food is excellent," I replied.

"I'm sure it is. And when exactly were you there, if I may ask?"

"I'm here right now, as a matter of fact," I said as I took a seat on a park bench across the street from the restaurant.

"I see. Well, my client appreciates that. I'm sure we'll be in touch," said Bigsby.

"I'll look forward to it," I said before disconnecting the call.

Well now. That proved that it came as a surprise to Pichter that his wife was on Catalina spending time with Carl. From that phone call, it didn't sound like Pichter was aware of what was going on under his nose with what were probably the two people he trusted most. Michelle was his wife, but Carl was his right-hand man in the protection of his family department. So what exactly was Jonathan Pichter thinking now? I wondered what kind of temper a man like Pichter had. He seemed cool, calm, and collected when I met him, but he's a big money power player in Hollywood, and this was a whole different set of circumstances. Something told me that I may have just opened a floodgate.

Then I got another text from Molly: "They're leaving." A moment later, I looked up to see Carl opening the door for Michelle and sidling up next her, arm around her waist as they strolled off down the street. I got up and followed from a safe distance after texting Molly back: "I'm on them. Go left out of the restaurant." They were heading toward the famed Avalon Casino and took a left turn as Molly caught up with me. She put her arm around me, and we both watched from a distance as they entered the exclusive Huntington Resort Hotel. Molly and I shared a look.

"What now?" she asked.

I told Molly about my text to Bigsby and the subsequent phone call. I pulled out my phone and texted Bigsby again: "It appears the couple is staying at the Huntington."

"You think it's wise, filling Jonathan Pichter in on all this?" Molly asked.

"I'm not sure. But if I'm going to pick sides, I'm going to pick Pichter. Something tells me we're in for some fireworks."

Bigsby texted back: "Understood. Thank you."

"So…?" Molly asked.

"So, let's go back to the boat. I think our work here is done for the evening," I said and gave Molly a kiss. We walked back to the water taxi dock arm in arm.

CHAPTER 20

When we got back to *Stella* I thought it would be better to take the money out of the Pelican case and stash it forward, under the V-berth. This would not only free up some space in the closet, it would also make it harder to grab the case and run if someone had a mind to. I stacked the piles under the spare mainsail, light wind jib, and spinnaker sail, hiding them from obvious view.

Satisfied with my work, I remade the V-berth when I heard Molly say, "Request permission to have an audience with the captain."

I turned to look at her and to my surprise, she stood before me wearing nothing but a smile and a floral sarong wrapped around her waist. I took in the sight with complete delight. She looked absolutely ravishing in the near darkness lit only by a soft cabin light.

"Permission granted," I smiled.

I felt myself stirring as she approached, seductively swinging her hips. She began silently undressing me, but when I tried to lean in to kiss her, she stopped me playfully by putting a finger to my lips while peeling off my shirt and rubbing her naked breasts against my bare chest. She bent down and licked my nipple as she unsnapped my jeans and pulled them down along with my boxers. As they fell to the floor, I climbed out of them, and Molly took me in her hand as she raised her head, kissing me deeply. She was driving me wild. I wrapped my arms around her, lifted her by her buttocks, turned her around, and planted her on the berth. I pulled the sarong off from around her waist and buried my face in her. Molly moaned in pleasure, running her hands through my hair as my tongue explored her. All I wanted to do was please her and it seemed to be working as she cried out and pushed herself into my face. She pulled me up by the hair and met my mouth deeply with her tongue. As we rolled over, Molly climbed aboard and took me. She sighed in pure pleasure as our bodies pulsated together. We became one again and looked into each other's eyes. Our bodies worked in rhythm, slowly at first, then working into a frenzy until we both cried out in sheer gratification, climaxing together. Molly collapsed in my arms, satiated and spent. We caressed each other gently as we basked in the moment, panting in satisfaction to catch our breaths, staring up at the star-filled sky through the forward hatch.

"You're fun," she said smiling between breaths.

"And you are so freakin' hot," I said with a shit-eating grin.

"I love being out here, on the water, floating," she said as she snuggled closer, putting her head on my chest.

"It is special, isn't it?"

"Is this how it was? I mean, when you sailed to Tahiti?"

"Well, I didn't have a beautiful woman like you with me."

She leaned up and faced me, asking, "You think I'm beautiful?"

"Hell, yeah, Molly. You know, I've always had the hots for you," I said.

"Really?"

"Yeah, really. Why? You don't believe me?"

"I guess I always felt there was some connection between us. It's just...I don't know. Jimmy never made me feel...I mean, at least not in a long time," she said.

"Hey, as far as I'm concerned, he's a fool for letting you go. But I'm very glad he did," I told her.

Molly smiled and kissed me. "You're sweet," she said.

"Just honest," I told her.

"Can we just stay like this? I mean, just sail away. See the world..."

"We can now. With the money." I said, thinking about the possibility though I'm not sure I really took her question seriously.

"Then let's do it," she said.

"You don't think you'd go stir crazy living on a small boat like this? Months on end? After your big place in Laurel Canyon?"

"No, I don't think I'd go crazy. It's cozy. You can be outside most of the time and have the ocean for your backyard."

"Well said," I agreed.

"And the whole world is there to explore. I think it would be a great adventure," she said, her face lighting up at the thought of it.

"I would think a woman your age would want to settle down more."

"Are you calling me old?"

"No, no. Not at all. It's just, you know, most woman your age..."

"Look, I'm not going to start a family at this stage in my life. I've been settled down for the past twenty years. All I've done is work to keep and make my home, and take an occasional vacation somewhere to lie on the beach. Maybe I need a little adventure in my life," she said. "Plus, after last night..." She paused. "I can't go back to what was. Things are different now. We could have been killed. It really made me realize my life can end at any time. It was an epiphany in a way. I need to do some living before I die."

"I know the feeling," I said.

"So let's do it!"

"You're serious, aren't you? I mean it's no small decision, packing up and leaving everything behind."

"What am I going to do if I stay? Work on another movie?

And after that, another? For what?! Live to pay my mortgage and take an occasional vacation?"

I smiled and nodded in agreement. She was making total sense to me. Plus I liked the idea of sailing off into the sunset with her.

"Besides," she continued, "I feel like I'll be looking over my shoulder all the time...waiting for when someone finds out..."

I leaned up on my elbow and looked her in the eye. "No one's going to find out."

"I want to leave it all behind. And I want to be with you," she said softly, looking straight into my eyes. "We're connected now."

She was drawing a hard bargain, but I felt the same way about her and said, "You're right. We are connected. And I want to be with you too." I meant every word of it. I leaned in and kissed her tenderly.

We talked some more and dreamt about the far-off places we could go and explore. Being realistic, I laid out what we would need to do if we were really going to make it work. We had enough money on board right now to keep us afloat for a number of years, even with the money I wanted to send to Rudy's sister. But we both had unfinished business back in town. Molly had to sell her house. I would also need to liquidate all my worldly assets like the Suburban, my furniture, all the stuff in my apartment. We would need to provision. I started making a mental list of all the maintenance, updates, and things for *Stella* we would need for a trip like that. But it was all possible and all doable. We eventually drifted off to sleep, our heads full of dreams of our future, wrapped in each other's arms.

The next morning I awoke early, let Molly sleep, and left her a note. I'd decided to make a quick run to the post office in town and get a box to send to Rudy's sister. I got to town and it was pretty quiet, with no sign of Carl, Michelle Bartley, or Jonathan

Pichter. I was early and had to wait for the post office to open, but promptly at 8:30 a.m., the doors opened, and I grabbed a couple of the largest flat-rate boxes they had. Without delay, I headed back to the water taxi dock and headed straight back to *Stella*. The water taxi dropped me off, and I climbed aboard *Stella* to the smell of coffee brewing and bacon frying.

"Ahoy, matey," I called down the companionway.

"Ahoy, captain", Molly called back. "I've got breakfast cooking," she said as I peered down below.

"So I see. Is that coffee I smell, too?"

"Aye aye," she replied, pouring me a mug.

I settled into the cockpit with my coffee while Molly continued with breakfast. I grabbed my binos and scanned the shoreline. I didn't see anyone familiar, but suddenly a corporate-looking helicopter circled the harbor a couple of times before heading toward the landing strip Catalina calls an airport. I wondered if it was Pichter coming to "straighten" things out.

Molly came up to the cockpit with breakfast of eggs and bacon and we ate in the morning sun. Afterwards, we jumped in the water for a morning swim then rinsed off in the shower. I wanted Molly to get the feel of what life on *Stella* would be like, and she seemed to really take to it, never complaining a bit. She already mastered the galley. She knew how to conserve precious fresh water by washing the dishes in salt water and only rinsing them in fresh. She'd even made the bunk and cleaned up by time I had returned. I thanked her.

"Nothing to it. I'm used to a two-and-half-thousand-square-foot house. This is a breeze," she replied.

"Well, so you know, I don't expect you to do all the dirty work," I told her.

"You better not, unless you want a mutiny on your hands," she joked.

"There'll be no talk like that, matey, or I'll have you flogged."

"Aye aye, captain. I meant it only in jest."

We laughed, and then I got down to packing the flat-rate

postal boxes with the wrapped bundles of cash. I stuffed as much as I could into each one until I reached four hundred grand spread out into three boxes. As an afterthought, I stuck a simple note inside each that read, "For Jenny, from Rudy," and sealed them up. I placed all the boxes into the empty Pelican case.

Molly was dressed and ready to hit town with me, so I called the water taxi for a pick-up. I scanned the shoreline once again for any signs of Carl, Michelle, or Pichter. Nothing.

When we got to shore, we went and rented a golf cart, the preferred method of transportation on the island. We drove straight to the post office. Inside, I took each box out of the Pelican case and handed them to the clerk. He took each one and asked if I had any liquids, hazardous materials, or lithium batteries inside.

I told him, "Nope, just paper items. Screenplays." It was the first thing I could think of.

"You're a screenwriter?"

"Well, I dabble," I lied.

"So, am I! But I really want to direct."

I smiled, held my tongue and nodded.

He looked down at the box he was holding. "Fort Myers, Florida?"

"Is there a problem?"

"Why would you be sending screenplays to Florida?"

"It's for a client. A producer. He's on location down there."

"Jennifer Whitley?" he said, reading the envelope.

"His assistant. Do you mind?"

"Hey, I'm just starting out and trying to make some connections. So, who's this producer? Somebody big?"

He was starting to annoy me. All I wanted to do was to get the boxes on their way.

Molly was beginning to smirk and trying hard to keep from laughing.

"I can't really say," I told him.

"Oh, yeah," he said a bit annoyed.

"Can I please pay and go, I'm late for a meeting," I told him.

"Sure. That'll be eighteen eighty-five, each," he said as he rang me up. "So your total is fifty-six fifty-five. Do you need any stamps today?"

"No, thanks," I said and handed him a hundred.

"Don't you want to put a return address?"

I hadn't put a return address on the boxes thinking if there weren't one it would *have* to get delivered to Jenny. But I didn't want to arouse any suspicion from the clerk, especially now that there were a couple of people in line behind me. I took back the boxes, borrowed his pen, and wrote down the first name that came to me: Al Phillips, the screenwriter who gave me the thumb drive with his screenplay on it. The same thumb drive I copied the Pays Lee pictures and video to. I didn't want to give my address, so I wrote down Pays Lee's office in Hollywood. I'd written out enough invoices to him to know it by heart.

"Al Phillips, Hollywood, huh?" said the clerk when I gave him back the boxes.

"Well, if you're going to be a screenwriter, where else are you going to live? Catalina?" I said, giving him a dig.

He shook his head agreeably, rang me up, and gave me my receipt, showing me how I could track my package online. I thanked him, grabbed Molly, and we headed out the door. By the time we got outside, Molly was laughing.

"Al Phillips?"

"Sure, he's a great screenwriter. Gonna be really big someday."

"Oh, I bet," she laughed.

"But he really wants to direct," I said.

We both cracked up about that.

Next stop was the hardware store. I went in to buy a shovel. I had an idea to bury the Pelican case. Maybe I was being overly paranoid, but I thought if Carl or anyone was watching us, they'd see us with the Pelican case, and I could claim I buried the money.

"You're not from around here, are you?" asked the tanned,

thin senior-aged proprietor when he checked out our shovel choice.

My paranoia was starting to make me wonder whether all these islanders were just being nosy, or if they were on to us. "Is that a problem?" I asked.

"No. We don't see many mainlanders coming here to buy shovels, that's all."

Again, I came up with something quick. "We're helping a friend with some landscaping. Except she doesn't have a shovel."

"Well, you know the ground's pretty hard and dry. You may want to grab a pickaxe too."

"Good idea," I said, now realizing he was simply trying to get us to spend more money in his shop. "What do you recommend?"

After showing us a couple of options, I picked out the most expensive one, which made the proprietor very happy.

Across the street was a sporting goods store I had seen the day before. We went in and bought a free-standing tent and a couple of sleeping bags.

We then packed the empty Pelican case, along with the shovel, pickaxe, tent, and sleeping bags onto the golf cart and headed inland, up the hill to the Hermit Gulch Campgrounds. We inquired at the ranger station about campsite availabilities along the upper edge near the trailhead. Being off-season, there were several sites available, so we took the furthest, most secluded site there was and paid the fee for three nights. We drove up to the site and unloaded. Luckily the campgrounds were quiet, and we got to work digging behind some thick bush that bordered our campsite.

Almost immediately I was glad the hardware store owner had talked us into buying the pickaxe. The ground was solid as rock, so I loosened the dirt with the pickaxe and Molly shoveled it out. We took turns and as each of us worked, the other kept an eye out for anybody watching. It took much longer than expected, but we finally dug a hole about three feet deep, big enough to fit the case. Once it was in, I took the shovel from Molly and covered the hole with loose dirt. We then pitched the tent over it to hide the fresh dig. Inside, we laid out the sleeping bags and stuffed the shovel and pickaxe in them. There were restrooms and showers at the campgrounds, so we were able to clean ourselves up before heading back to town.

We returned the golf cart and idled the rest of the day strolling around Avalon, had a late leisurely lunch then afternoon cocktails. We kept our eyes peeled for Michelle, Carl, or Pichter, scoping out each place before we entered. Nothing. We decided to call it an early evening and go back to fix dinner aboard *Stella*. As we were heading for the water taxi dock, two L.A. County sheriff deputy SUVs blew by us with their lights and sirens on. They were headed in the direction of the Huntington Resort. My curiosity got the better of me, and I stopped.

I turned to Molly and said, "Come on, let's see where they're heading."

"You think it has something to do with...?" She left it hanging.

I shrugged my shoulders unsure either way, but when we turned off Crescent Avenue and down to the Huntington, we could see the vehicles outside the entrance as a third patrol vehicle pulled up. Deputies emerged and ran into the hotel. Molly and I exchanged looks and immediately turned back. We hurried for the water taxi dock as a fourth police SUV flew by, sirens blaring.

"Something's going on."

"Oh, my God," was all Molly could mutter.

When we got to the water taxi dock, we sat and watched as an ambulance drove by. Molly squeezed my hand and gave me a nervous look. The crusty taxi dispatcher came out of his hut, lit up a Lucky Strike, nodded toward the ambulance, and looked to us.

"Seems like somebody got killed at the Huntington. Just heard it on the police scanner," he said matter-of-factly.

"Killed! Wow," I said. "They say who it was?"

"Some actress, or singer, or something from what I gather."

Molly and I exchanged looks as she squeezed my hand again and buried her head into my arm.

"I guess it must be somebody famous. They got the whole force heading over there," he said.

"You catch the name?" I asked.

"They mentioned it, but I don't follow them people," he said bitterly then spit into the water.

We looked off in the direction of the Huntington, both trying to imagine what was going on when the water taxi pulled up.

"Here's your ride," said the dispatcher, picking loose tobacco from his lips.

"Thanks," I said. I got up and helped a shaken Molly to her feet.

"Guess the TV crews will be heading over if this lady was somebody big. You know, I was on TV when that one actor drowned a few years back. I forget his name."

"Oh, yeah?" I answered trying to sound interested, but moving down the ramp to the water taxi. But he kept going.

"You bet. They interviewed me. Was in all the papers too. Spelled my damn name wrong though." He exhaled a cloud of smoke and tossed his butt in the water.

As we got on the water taxi, the driver rolled his eyes at the dispatcher, and confirmed we were heading to mooring 57. He'd gotten some generous tips from us and remembered where we were going.

When we got back to *Stella,* I turned on the radio and tuned into the all-news station. They hadn't picked anything up yet, and I imagined the Sheriff's Department in Avalon was trying to keep things quiet. That was somewhat easier to do here on Catalina than on the mainland. From the cockpit, we could see the flashing lights of the patrol vehicles bouncing off the nearby buildings, but we didn't have a clear view of the Huntington. The police lights stayed on for a long time, and as the sun set it seemed like even more of a calamity. Neither of us felt like eating, but we both threw back some bourbon, trying to make sense of what was going on back on shore.

"You think it was Michelle Bartley?" Molly finally asked.

"Well, I guess there could be another singer actress staying there, but what are the chances?"

"I feel like we could be responsible," she said.

"Why? We didn't kill her."

"I know, but we got word to her husband that, you know, Carl was with her. I mean, should we tell the police?"

I grabbed Molly by the arm and spun her around to face me.

"Molly, going to the police is the last thing we want to do. Understand?"

"Of course," she said nodding her head.

"We don't know what happened over there, and we sure as hell don't want to get involved. I think you know why. Right?"

"Right, right. I don't know what I was thinking. I was feeling like maybe we…"

"*We* had nothing to do with it," I stressed.

"You're right, I'm sorry."

"Listen to me, Molly. From here on in, we've got to fly under the radar. We don't want to call any attention to ourselves. We've got to avoid the police or any attention at all costs. We don't want to have to answer any questions. So far, we're in the clear of all that's happened to us. We need to keep it that way."

"Yes, I get it. I'm sorry."

I put my arms around her and pulled her into a hug.

"I'm sorry, I understand your feelings. But we have to be careful and look out for ourselves."

"I know," she said and grew silent.

"You okay?" I asked, lifting her chin to look her in the eyes.

She nodded, leaned in, and gave me a kiss.

We sat in the cockpit for a long time, listening to the local and national news along with the weather and L.A. traffic reports. It all seemed so far away on this quiet night in Avalon

Harbor as we sat with our eyes glued to the shore, sipping bourbon. There was still nothing on the radio about any death in Avalon and no mention on any of the news apps on my phone. The police vehicle lights eventually went out, but every once in a while, we'd see one race down Crescent Avenue, lights on but no siren. It got late, and we decided to turn in.

We lay awake for some time, not saying anything and just staring up at the stars out through the open fore hatch. I kept thinking about what Molly had said and how maybe I *was* responsible for Michelle Bartley's death. If that even *was* who got killed. I hoped by some chance there was another famous singer staying at the Huntington who was the victim. But the more I ran it through my head, the more I knew it had to be Michelle Bartley.

I could tell Molly was still pretty shaken up about it. She rested her head on my chest, and, I couldn't see her face, but a couple of times I thought she might be crying. I started to wonder if I'd been too harsh with her, the way I told her we couldn't go to the police. But I knew I was right. This was another secret we had between us that we had to take to our graves. I hoped she didn't blame me for Michelle Bartley's death, if in fact it was her. But in some respect, I was blaming myself.

Could Pichter be so cold to have killed his wife? The same woman whose life he literally saved? I didn't think so at first, but one thing I've learned in Hollywood is to not be surprised by anything. He sure as hell wasn't the kind of person to do it himself. Who did he get to do his dirty work this time? All these thoughts were winding around in my head until I finally drifted off.

CHAPTER 21

I awoke sometime later, sensing movement on the boat. I sat up, stirring Molly as I saw a figure climbing down the companionway from the cockpit. I instinctively reached for my marine shotgun but remembered the Santa Monica P.D had confiscated it. I thought about Swanzy's .40 caliber but remembered I had left it in the cockpit. Suddenly, the cabin lights came on and I saw it pointing at me. It was held by a dripping wet, stripped to his waist figure—Carl. Molly yelped at the sight.

"So, you killed Swanzy..." he said.

"We didn't kill anybody!" I replied.

"I don't give a shit if you did or not. I just want the money."

"What money...?" I barely got it out before he pistol-whipped me with the butt of the gun, cutting a gash in my cheek and laying me out on the V-berth.

"Stop!" Molly screamed as she threw herself over me, trying to protect me and dabbing my wound with her sarong.

"Let's get something straight, we're not going to play this game. I saw you take the money, so let's dispense with the bullshit. I was there, at the airport that night. I just want to know if it's here on the boat."

"What's he talking about?" Molly played dumb.

"Swanzy took the money," I said.

"Then where is he?" Carl asked.

"He jumped ship! Took my dinghy and got picked up by some

other boat," I lied, trying to make up a semi-believable story.

Carl pulled me away from Molly and whacked me again upside my head with the butt.

"Stop!" screamed Molly.

"Then what am I doing with his gun in my hand?"

"That's not his…"

"Bullshit! I know it is because I got it for him."

Rubbing my head, I looked up at him and tried to call his bluff. "You weren't there."

"Yeah, I was. I had to make sure Swanzy completed the job. But I wasn't going to let that idiot walk away with all that money." He then pointed the gun at Molly. "Now you got about three seconds to tell me where it is or I blow your little honey away right here."

"No, wait!" I tried to stall.

"Give him what he wants!" yelled Molly.

"One…" he started counting.

"Wait!"

"Two…"

"Mike…!" cried Molly.

"Okay, okay, I'll tell you," I said.

He looked at me but kept the gun on Molly. "I'm going to make it three."

"Tell him!" said Molly.

"It's on the island. I buried it."

"What?!"

"You heard me. I buried it. You know, like a pirate. Buried treasure."

"Why the hell would you bury it?"

"In case someone broke into the boat while we were ashore. I didn't feel good about leaving it aboard."

"Are you fucking kidding me? You got a treasure map too?" he said.

"I don't need a map."

"Okay, she'll show me where it is," he said.

"What money? I don't know what you're talking about." Molly shot me a look, playing the part well. I tried to play the guilty party.

"She doesn't know anything about it. Or where it is. I'll show you."

Carl thought about it a minute looking around the cabin, opening cabinets, searching.

"It's not here," I said.

He found my roll of duct tape and threw it at me as he continued to search.

"Tie her up," he said nodding at Molly.

I taped Molly's wrists as we stared into each other's eyes, desperately trying to silently communicate with each other. I kept shifting my eyes toward the shelf in the V-berth where my diving knife was, hoping she got the message. With a little luck, she should be able to retrieve it with her foot and free herself.

Carl continued to search as I got done with her wrists and told me to tape up her ankles as well. As I did that, Carl pulled out an extra line I had coiled and hanging in one of the lockers. He undid the coil, tied it around the mast and brought the line over to Molly and told me to secure her wrists below the tape. I did what I was told and kept indicating the direction of my knife with my eyes to Molly. She glanced over in the direction confused but when she looked back at me I gave her an indiscrete nod. Carl rummaged around my cabinets and pulled out some clothes I had in there. He tossed an old bandana at me.

"Gag her. And use the tape," he ordered.

As gently as I could, I stuffed the bandana in Molly's mouth and wrapped the tape around her head, trying my best to make her as comfortable as I could, all the time trying to apologize to her with my eyes.

"I'm sorry, Molly," I whispered. "I am so sorry."

As Molly laid in the V-berth, bound and gagged, I blew her a kiss and saw a tear run down her cheek.

"Let's go, lover boy," Carl barked.

I checked my watch and told him the water taxi won't be running for another three hours.

"Yeah, well, we ain't waiting. We're swimming," he said.

"But I can't swim," I lied, not too convincingly, trying to buy time.

"Well, you're going to learn fast or drown." He waved the pistol toward the companionway. "Let's go," Carl barked.

"Let me get my wetsuit at least."

All I had on were my boxer shorts and a T-shirt, so I reached for the locker I kept it in.

"Forget it," as he shoved me toward the stairs.

I looked back at Molly once again. She stared at me wide-eyed, scared and anxious. I mouthed, "I love you" and blew her a kiss. Carl turned the cabin lights offs and forced me up on deck with the barrel of the gun.

In the cockpit, Carl paused to let his eyes adjust to the darkness. He looked off at one of our mooring neighbors and saw an inflatable dinghy tied to the stern.

"Go get that Zodiac. Try anything stupid, and I kill the girl, got it?"

"But I told you, I can't swim."

"Cut the bullshit and go get that Zodiac."

With that Carl pushed with one hand, pistol in the ribs with the other and shoved me into the water. It was cold and like a slap in the face. The cut on my cheek stung from the salt water, and my head throbbed from where he'd whacked me. I immediately started swimming toward the dinghy, trying to warm up. It was only about thirty yards away, but it felt like it took me forever to get to it.

When I finally made it, I clambered into it and untied it from the pleasure yacht it was secured to. The cool night air had me shivering as soon as I was out of the water. There were a couple of paddle oars in the boat, and I started rowing straight away, again trying to generate some warmth. I didn't like the idea of Carl alone on *Stella* with Molly and rowed as fast as I could to pick him up. Luckily he waited for me in the cockpit, watching me, making sure I didn't try anything while he changed into my dry sweatshirt and linen pants.

As I pulled up alongside of *Stella*, Carl hopped in with Swanzy's gun trained on me.

"Not bad for someone who can't swim."

I shrugged and starting rowing, struggling to keep warm and fight the shivers. I studied him as I rowed and tested the waters, "So you killed Michelle?"

"Shut up!" he snapped. "I didn't kill anyone."

"Then why you running from the police?"

"Who's running?" he said, trying to sound cool, calm and collected.

"Oh, just out for a moonlight swim with all your clothes on, huh?

"I found you and wanted to get my money."

"*Your* money?" I asked.

"That's right. Mine now."

"I see," I said, still shivering. "So you were doing it for her, but then you figured you could keep the whole thing if you killed her."

"I told you, I didn't kill her!" He looked off toward the Huntington as we got closer to the beach.

I pulled a few more strokes before egging him on. "So, were you banging her?"

He shot me an angry look. I pushed on.

"I saw you two together, in the restaurant last night. You looked pretty cozy."

"You were in the restaurant...?" Carl studied me. "You don't know shit."

"Hey, I know what I saw."

Carl shook his head, "It was strictly business."

"Okay, if that's what you want to call it."

"We were there to meet Swanzy and get the money."

"Now you don't have to split it. That why she's dead now?"

"Pichter must have had her followed. She's been trying to get away from that son-of-a-bitch for some time. I was trying to help," Carl said.

"A real boy scout, huh?"

"Shut the fuck up!" he snapped angrily.

I pulled hard once more and then drifted to the beach. "You know, they'll pin it on you whether you did it or not."

Carl glared at me, but I'd gotten him thinking. I think he suspected I was right.

We came to a halt as the dinghy ran into the sand. Carl immediately got up and pulled me to my feet, jabbing the barrel of the pistol into my still sore ribs.

"Where we going?" he asked.

"Up the hill, by the campgrounds," I pointed.

"Let's go," he nudged.

The streets were dark and quiet now. I was still wet and cold, my gashed cheek was beginning to swell and now I was looking at a long walk in bare feet. It seemed like there was still some activity down near the Huntington. Carl eyed it as he led me hobbling across the street, and we started up the hill. Passing the golf course it was slow going, the hard ground, stones, and pebbles were incredibly painful on my feet, but I wanted to keep Carl talking.

"You said you were at the airport that night. Did you arrange for Swanzy to kill Pays Lee?"

"I was there to make sure the job got done."

"So Pichter arranged it."

"I told you, you don't know shit."

Then I remembered what Swanzy said. If Michelle had seen those pictures on Lauren's phone…

"Michelle! *She* put him up to it. Swanzy would have done anything for her."

"Think you're pretty smart, huh?"

"Doesn't take a genius. I'd assumed it was Pichter protecting her."

201

"Let me tell you something, Mister Fucking Genius, Pays Lee and his enterprise were worth way too much for Pichter to lose him. The last thing he wanted was to see Pays Lee dead. Hell, Pichter was paying Pays to keep quiet."

"Keep quiet about what?"

"Plenty."

"You mean, like Pays Lee being Lauren's father?" I kept pushing, trying to keep Carl going.

"Swanzy tell you that?"

I nodded. "I could see why Pichter would want to keep that quiet. The father of Michelle's child, fucking her child. The scandal mongers would love that."

"That. And her comeback album. That was another reason. It was all fucking hush-hush."

"Michelle was making a comeback album?"

Carl nodded, "Yeah. Pays Lee was producing it. Michelle never sounded better. Was going to re-ignite her career. But when Pichter found out Michelle was sleeping with Pays Lee again, he pulled the plug."

"What?" The shit was getting deep.

"Yeah, Pichter was pissed. Confiscated all the digital files from the studio and locked them away. He's made Michelle's life a living hell ever since."

I stumbled along, shivering, feet getting cut up, as I tried to put it all together.

"I don't understand. Why would Pichter pay Pays Lee to keep quiet about all this? Seems like he'd be the one to have Pays Lee bumped off."

"Because, dumb shit, Pays Lee is a huge money train for Pichter, and for a bunch of his clients. He was making ten-fold of the cash he was paying Pays to keep quiet."

We walked on, Carl pushing me. I was still trying to digest everything that he had told me. It was slow going as my feet were getting worn raw from the rough asphalt. We still had a way to go, and I wanted him to keep talking.

"So, wait, how did Michelle find out about Pays Lee and Lauren?"

"Doesn't matter. Now shut up."

We shuffled on a bit more before I chimed in, "You grabbed the phone from me. *You* showed her!"

"No, I delivered it to Pichter, as ordered. Like I said, he made Michelle's life a living hell."

"Pichter showed her the pictures on Lauren's phone?"

"And the video. Nice guy, huh?"

"Damn," was all I could say. What a story.

We were getting up to the campground. All the lights were out, and it was pitch black.

"Where the fuck are we going?" demanded Carl.

"Not much further, I think."

"You *think*?!"

"Hey, it wasn't dark when I came up here before."

We walked through the grounds toward our campsite.

"Up here," I pointed and led the way.

It was even rougher walking on the rocky dirt trail barefooted. My feet were torn up and bloodied but Carl kept nudging me on with a pistol jab every time I slowed down. We finally made it to the campsite, and I pointed to the tent.

"Here, under the tent." I pointed to the ground.

He kicked the tent a few feet over then pointed with the pistol and said, "Start digging."

I went to open the tent to get the shovel but Carl stopped me. "Hold it."

"The shovel's in the sleeping bag," I told him.

He motioned with the pistol for me to step away so I did. He kept his eyes and the gun on me as he felt around in the tent, then pulled out the shovel and threw it at my feet.

"Don't try anything funny."

"What happens when I give you the money? You going to kill me?" I asked.

"Once I get the money, I got no beef with you," he said.

"How do you know I won't go to the police?" I asked.

"What are you going to tell them? That you were at the airport that night and stole the money off Pays Lee? That you went and stashed the money before you called the police to report the murder? That you killed Swanzy when he tried to get the money back?"

"I didn't kill…"

"Save it," he cut me off. "You're in this as deep as I am. You're not going to the police."

I nodded. It was hard to argue the point, but I was still certain he'd kill me once he had the money. Clean up loose ends. That's what guys like him do. Maybe he'd even somehow blame me for Michelle's death. But I wanted him to think I believed him, and I wanted to warm up, so I started digging.

The sky was getting lighter as the sun started to rise when I hit the Pelican case. Carl heard the shovel connect and I could see him smile as I continued to dig it out. He had me toss the shovel away so I could pull the case from its grave. I hauled it out, placing in in front of him. He waved me away with the pistol and got down on his knees to open it. As he undid the latches I sat down next to the tent and reached in for the pickaxe.

He opened it. When he saw it was empty, he turned toward me with the pistol.

"What the f…"

But I had the pickaxe. I jumped up and swung it broadly at him. He ducked back, and I hit him in his arm just as he pulled the trigger, firing, narrowly missing me. The gun went flying, and he lunged at me. Swinging the pickaxe back in the opposite direction I connected with the side of his head and he went down. I looked briefly for the gun but couldn't see it. As Carl struggled to his knees rubbing his head, I swung the pickaxe again, this time hitting him in his ribs. He spun over on his back reeling in pain.

I got down on my hands and knees and felt around, searching for the gun. When I couldn't find it, I decided to make a run for it. I got back to my feet and was about to run when Carl tackled me from behind. We rolled around in the dirt, wrestling, gouging, and trying to land punches on each other. Carl overpowered me and got on top, straddling me, putting me in a chokehold. I tried to wriggle away and punch my way out of it, but he was not letting go. I tried prying his hands off, but they were like vices, locked in a death grip. Gasping for breath, I felt myself going. My vision was fading. I couldn't believe this was happening to me again, and this time Molly wasn't around to save the day. In a last ditch effort, I reached around the ground around me and felt a good sized rock. I grabbed it, conjured up my last bit of strength, and brought it down onto his temple with all my might, or at least what was left of it. It was enough. He fell off me, and I gasped for air, struggling to get to my feet. I went for the pickaxe, but Carl came up with the gun. He fired, hitting my hand as I reached for the handle. I spun around in pain, grabbing the pickaxe in my other hand and in a feeble attempt, threw it at Carl. It was enough for him to duck out of its way as I took off down the rocky hill. I heard the crack of another gunshot and felt the bullet whiz by my ear.

My raw, torn, bare feet were screaming as I ran. My hand was bleeding badly, but I knew I couldn't stop. As I ran by the ranger campsite registration station, I banged loudly on the door. I saw a light come on inside and heard another gunshot. The bullet hit the building with a loud report, splintering the wooden siding. I called out to whoever was inside to call the sheriff, and took off running again. I heard a couple more shots but kept running as fast as my adrenaline-induced bare feet would, down the road, trying to ignore the pain.

I was all the way down near the golf course when I finally saw the deputy sheriff's car come racing up the canyon road toward me with lights flashing.

I ducked off the road to avoid him and collapsed onto the fairway, heaving to catch my breath as the patrol car flew by. I lay in the wet grass unable to move from pain and exhaustion. I was struggling to catch my breath, and my hand screamed in pain. The bullet had gone right through my palm between my thumb and forefinger. I held my hand to my chest rolled in my wet T-shirt and closed my eyes, trying to gather some strength for my next move. My feet were on fire and the soft wet grass felt good beneath them. I knew I should get up and go, but I felt as if I couldn't move. I was paralyzed and just wanted to lie there and go to sleep. I knew this was not a good sign, but I couldn't shake myself out of it. As my breathing calmed and the adrenaline started to fade, the cool night air and dewy wet grass sent a shiver down my spine. It brought me back again to that winter day in The Bronx when that icy drop from the elevated IRT train nailed me right on the back of my neck. That jolted me awake and back to reality. But when I opened my eyes, Carl was there, standing over me pointing the gun at my face. His face was bloodied from where I hit him with the rock.

"I going to fucking kill you, and then I'm going back to your boat, and I'm going to kill your girlfriend."

At that moment I knew I was going to die. There was nothing I could do about it. "Fuck you!" I spit out defiantly. It was all I could come up with to say. I struggled to get up expecting death at any moment when suddenly—

"Drop it! Sheriff's department," a voice rang out.

A spotlight hit Carl, and he instinctively raised the gun toward the light. A shot rang out and his chest exploded. Blood splattered my face as he went down beside me, clutching his chest. I pulled myself away from him as the deputies ran up and trained their guns on him speaking into their walkie-talkies.

"We've had shots fired and have two down. We're going to need an ambulance."

Once they secured Carl's gun and made sure he was no longer a threat, one of the deputies finally turned to me and shined his flashlight in my face. I was covered in blood and he asked, "You okay?"

Something about the ridiculousness of the question, the

emotional roller coaster of the near death experience I'd just been through, and the culmination of the last couple of days made me start to laugh. All I could do was lie there laughing, as I clutched my bleeding hand and watched Carl fight for his life, squirming in the grass.

CHAPTER 22

Muddied, bloodied, and bruised, the deputies put a tourniquet around my arm and stuffed dressing into the hole in my hand wiping any smile or sense of laughter from my face as I screamed in pain. Wrapping me in a blanket, they put me in the same ambulance as Carl. I watched as the EMTs worked feverishly to save his life. He didn't look like he was going to make it, but what did I know? When we arrived at the hospital, they rushed Carl off on a gurney and disappeared down the hall.

They put me on a wheelchair and wheeled me into surgery, knocked me out, and worked on my hand for over four hours. When I woke up they told me the bullet went right through the fleshy part between my thumb and forefinger, and that I was lucky not to lose the hand or any of my digits. They had bandaged it all up to the size of a softball. The cut on my cheek took a couple of stitches, and they patched up and bandaged my feet.

As I lay in the recovery room, a deputy came in and started getting my statement. All I could think about was Molly, still tied up on the boat. But I wanted to keep her out of it as long as I could, so I didn't mention anything about her—or the money. How long had she been there like that? I'd lost track of time and had to think of something fast to tell the deputy. I tried to play groggy, which wasn't too hard, and told him that Carl abducted me from my boat and dragged me ashore with the sole purpose of killing me. I tried to be as vague as possible, knowing full well that the detectives would come in for the details and make me repeat the story many times, like Gomez and Lo did. When asked why Carl would want to kill me, I told him I wasn't sure but I'd seen him and Michelle Bartley at the Casa del Mar the night before. I explained that I had met him once before, and he must have recognized me when he was in the restaurant with Michelle. The deputy seemed to buy it that I could link him to Michelle. He told me what I already knew, that detectives would want to question me as well.

Once the deputy left and things quieted down, I struggled out of bed and pulled out the intravenous tube from my arm. With my bandaged feet, I tiptoed down the hall and ducked into a sort of locker room. Inside there were neatly stacked piles of doctor's scrubs, so I pulled off my hospital gown and got dressed. I found some slippers and draped an extra scrubs shirt over my bandaged hand to hide it. Once I was ready, I headed out of the locker room, strode down the hall the best could without limping, and out the door like I owned the place.

I limped down to the water taxi dock and talked the driver into giving me a free ride since I didn't have any money on me. Tipping him well the last few days paid off. He eyed my outfit and my hospital I.D. bracelet, which I had neglected to remove, and asked if I was okay. I assured him I was, but I don't think he was buying it.

The driver helped me aboard when we pulled up beside *Stella*, and I thanked him profusely. He didn't have any other passengers and hung out until I got the companionway open. I called inside, "Molly?" then went down below. But Molly was nowhere to be seen, along with any evidence of her ever being there. Her clothes, the duct tape, the dirty dishes, everything had been cleaned up and cleaned out. I was stunned. I couldn't believe it. But I also breathed a sigh of relief, happy Molly had been able to free herself.

The water taxi driver shouted from his boat and asked if I was looking for my girlfriend. I popped my head back out the companionway doorway to see he was still beside *Stella*, and said, yeah, I was. He told me he had picked her up a couple of hours before and saw her heading over to the ferry station. I looked out across the bay and saw the morning ferry heading back to the mainland. I thanked the driver again and went for my phone so I could call her. I had left it on the shelf in the forward V-berth but when I looked for it, it was gone. I searched around the V-berth and then the rest of boat to no avail. Molly must have taken it or gotten rid of it. That had to be it. The more I thought about it, what with the text messages and photos on it, the more I gave Molly credit for getting rid of it. With no phone, the police couldn't tie us together or see what I had texted to Bigsby.

The money? I went back to the V-berth, lifted the mattress, and pulled out the spare sails. The money was gone too. I tried to wrap my head around what might have happened. Obviously Molly must have taken it. Was she cleaning things up in preparation for an investigation? Did she think I was dead? Or was she running off with the money?

I didn't want to believe my last thought. I threw on some clothes and eased my achy, bandaged feet into some boat shoes. I knew I'd never be able to catch the ferry but I wouldn't be too far behind if I left right away. But as I got up on deck, the sheriff's boat was pulling up.

"Going somewhere, Mister Millek?" barked the deputy over the loudspeaker.

By time we pulled up to the sheriff's dock, I was getting my story straight. When I got inside the station, as I suspected, the detectives put me in an interrogation room that was little more than a small office. Probably had a previous life as a closet. They asked me for my phone, and I was happy I didn't have it. I told them it was gone. I told them Carl must have tossed it overboard when he abducted me. I told them how he dragged me up to the campgrounds because he said he wanted to kill me. When they asked me why, I stuck to my previous story and explained how I met Carl through Jonathan Pichter, Michelle Bartley's husband. Carl saw me when he was with Michelle at Casa del Mar, so he knew I had seen them together. He must have been trying to be incognito about it and thought I blew his cover. Obviously he killed Michelle and was now coming after me so there wouldn't be any witnesses to identify him. The detectives took copious notes, and I imagined they'd be checking my story out with the Casa del Mar wait staff.

They questioned me at length as to why I was in Avalon in the first place and why had I rented a camping site when I had a boat to sleep on. I told them that I was planning on doing some hiking and felt like camping out so I could get an early start. They asked why there was a hole dug and an empty Pelican case, but I pleaded ignorance about the case and said that Carl made me dig the hole, thinking he was going to kill and bury me. I was surprised they didn't ask me about Molly because it sounded like they already had gotten a statement from the camp ranger. He must have told them there were two of us, unless he was too freaked out from the shooting to have bothered mentioning it. Besides, I didn't think I was any kind of suspect, so they were probably concentrating their investigation on getting all the facts about Carl's story straight.

Later in the afternoon, word came in that Carl didn't make it, and they left me alone for what felt like an hour. Just as I thought, and probably with my help, they pinned Michelle's murder on him. After all, he had checked into the Huntington with her, plus they found his knife, which was apparently used to slit her throat. It was all working itself out neat and tidy for the detectives. And for Jonathan Pichter. I didn't want to complicate things by adding anything to my story that didn't help wrap up the case with a nice ribbon and bow.

Finally one of the detectives came in and told me that a couple of deputies were taking me back to the hospital. I tried to protest but they were not having any of it.

"Why were you trying to leave the island?" the lead detective asked me.

"I wasn't," I said and held up my bandaged hand. I told him I was in no shape to sail anywhere.

"Then why'd you break out of the hospital in the first place?"

"Everything I own is on my boat and I wanted to make sure it was okay. And I wanted to get my phone, but it was gone."

They seemed to accept that. But, they explained, because I'd had major surgery, I was required to stay at the hospital at least overnight for observation. Liability issues, I guessed. And then, if I wanted to, and got the doctors' okay, I could officially check myself out tomorrow.

When I got back to the hospital, there were a bunch of reporters outside and the deputies had to escort me through the crowd while they shouted questions at me. I pulled my shirt over my head like a fugitive to hide my identity. Cameras and microphones were shoved in my face as I walked the gauntlet. The last thing I wanted to do was talk to reporters or get my face in the papers.

I thought I saw someone and as I got inside, I turned and looked back at the crowd outside through the glass door. There, standing tall behind the gathered reporters was a face I recognized. It was Butch, the guy who Pays Lee wanted me to leave Lauren with the night he left me with her. Our eyes met for a brief moment before he turned and disappeared behind the crowd. I had to wonder why he was there. It could not have been merely a coincidence.

That evening in the hospital, I watched the TV news coverage of Michelle Bartley's murder and the sheriff's deputy shooting of her killer. I heard myself referred to by name only as a witness and second victim, expected to survive. There was a phone in the room, and I tried calling Molly several times, both on her cell and at her home number. The first couple of calls, I left vague messages telling her where I was and asking her to call. But when I called again later on after not hearing back from her, I got a recording that her number was no longer in service.

The next morning I checked out as soon as I could, which

wasn't until noon after getting the doctor's reluctant okay and dealing with the paperwork. There were still a couple of reporters hanging around outside, but I managed to avoid them and kept an eye out for Butch. He was nowhere to be seen, and I was okay with that. On the way back to *Stella*, I asked the water taxi captain if by chance he had seen Molly again. He told me he hadn't since he picked her up yesterday morning. I thanked him and gave him my last twenty as a tip.

Back aboard *Stella*, I went straight to the V-berth, lifted the mattress and pulled out the spare sails. I don't know why, but I had to look again. The money was still gone. Not that I thought it would be back, but I had to check. I tried harder to find some message Molly might have left me. I tore everything apart, searching for some sign, but there wasn't any.

I decided to wait there aboard *Stella* for the rest of the day, hoping she would come back. Had she gotten my messages? Would she know that I had checked out of the hospital? I flew from the spreaders the colorful windsock we'd bought on our shopping excursion, thinking that if she saw it, she'd know I was aboard. I scanned the crowds at the ferry dock with my binoculars with each arrival from the mainland. I was probably being naïve, but I was still holding out that she would come back. Hoping that she had not run off on me.

My hand was hurting so I popped a couple of the painkillers they gave me at the hospital and crashed out around sunset. I slept most of the night and awoke to still no Molly. I made some coffee and waited for the sun to rise. When it did, I started the engine, dropped the mooring line and motored out of the bay. When I hit open water, I raised the main and managed to unfurl the jib, giving a new definition of being singlehanded. My hand was still throbbing, though now in a dull aching pain, so I popped a couple more painkillers and motor-sailed straight back for Marina del Rey.

CHAPTER 23

I half-hoped to see Molly on the dock as I pulled *Stella* into my slip back at the marina, but there was no sign of her. The whole way back from Catalina I kept replaying the last time we were together in my head to try and get a clue as to where Molly might have gone or how she might try to contact me. Could she be furious with me for getting her into this whole mess? For risking her life and for her killing Swanzy? For getting her almost killed again by Carl? And why? All because of the money, money that I kept from her until Swanzy came into the picture.

When I got to my apartment, I fired up my laptop and sent Molly an email but it came back almost immediately as "address undeliverable." I hadn't had a landline in years so I went to Liz's rental office and asked if I could make a quick call, explaining that I had lost my phone. After answering questions and making up an accident story about my bandaged hand and cheek, I called Molly's cell then her home number. Both were now disconnected and no longer in service.

No longer very optimistic but with nowhere else to go, I fought the late afternoon rush-hour traffic and drove over to Laurel Canyon. There in front of Molly's house was a banner reading "Sold!" on the realtor's For Sale sign. I rang the bell several times then banged on the door.

"Molly, are you in there? Open up, it's me, Mike," I shouted.

"Can I help you?" came a voice from behind me.

I turned to see a smartly dressed, middle-aged woman emerge from the side gate.

"Yes, I'm looking for the owner, or, er, previous owner I guess. Molly. Molly Sheehan."

"I'm sorry but she moved out yesterday. As soon as she signed the sale agreement, she grabbed a few things and told me to contact her husband to get rid of the rest," she said.

"You mean her ex-husband?" I told her.

"Yes, I suppose that's correct," she said. I got the hint of an attitude.

I decided to play nice and extended my good hand in hopes of getting some info from her. "I'm sorry, my name is Mike. I'm Molly's brother."

"Barbara Bayner, Canyon Realty," she said.

"I just got back in town, had an accident and lost my phone. Did Molly leave a forwarding address or number?"

"No, she didn't."

I thought she might be holding out so I made up a sob story in hopes she would come clean. "You see, our mother is in a home, and she fell this morning, broke her hip. Molly's got power of attorney and the do not resuscitate order. They need it at the hospital in order for Mom to get her surgery."

"Oh, my, I'm so sorry," she said.

"Thank you. These things happen. Mom's ninety-one. So, do you have any idea where I might find my sister?"

"I wish I did. But if I hear from her where can I tell her your mother is?"

I was afraid I wasn't getting anywhere with Babs. I believed she didn't know so I went back to the Suburban.

"Marina Hospital, in Marina del Rey. She'll know it. Thank you," I said, and I hopped in and drove off.

At a loss, I picked up a bottle of bourbon on the way back to the marina and decided to drown my sorrows. Things were not looking good.

Back in my apartment I poured myself a stiff one, popped a

couple more painkillers, swallowed them with the bourbon, and then poured another. I drank the night away, replaying our last few days in my head. All we'd been through, the thought of Molly, our lovemaking, our connection, and our plan to sail off into the sunset, all of it played over and over. She had given me the hope of a new life, with a real partner, with someone I finally felt close to. I thought I felt that way with Sandy, years ago, but there was always a distance between us, even when we were close. With Molly, I'd finally found a real bond, maybe even true happiness. Or so I thought. Was it all a dream? Did I just imagine it all? The idea of losing her was breaking my heart.

I passed out on the couch and woke up to a pounding in my head. Only it wasn't in my head but on my front door. I got up and staggered to the door, my bandaged feet stinging. I opened it to find Santa Monica's finest, Gomez and Lo.

"Can we come in?" asked Lo as they walked right by me into the living room.

"You look like shit, Millek." It was Gomez this time.

"Yeah, well, I haven't had my coffee yet," I said as I shuffled to the kitchen to make some.

"Why are there more and more dead bodies showing up wherever you go?" asked Lo.

"Don't you know by now, I'm the Angel of Death. You probably don't want to be hanging around me too long. Coffee?" I pulled out some clean mugs from the cupboard and went about brewing a pot.

"So what do you know about this guy, Carl Brandt?" asked Gomez.

It was the first time I had heard Carl's last name and had to think about it.

"Carl? Nothing. I mean, I knew he worked for Jonathan Pichter. He drove me home that night you guys tried to hold me. I guess it turns out he was banging Pichter's wife. Apparently she screwed him over somehow, and he killed her. Then he came after me."

"Why you?" asked Lo.

"I happened to see him and Michelle Bartley together that day on Catalina. They looked real...cozy, if you catch my drift. He must have seen me and knew I could tie them together."

"I thought we told you not to leave town," barked Lo.

"I didn't. Catalina is still part of L.A. County."

"So you ratted him out to his boss?" said Gomez, pushing me to continue.

"Yeah. Yeah, I did. I figured I owed Pichter something for bailing me out of your jail that night. Figured he'd want to know about it. We had a nice talk on the way back to my place that night. How he was so concerned about protecting his family. So, when I saw something that might have been a threat to his family, I wanted to help. Why are you so interested in Carl anyway? He's dead."

"The gun he had with him was a .40 caliber. Ballistics matched it to the gun that killed Pays Lee, his bodyguard, and your friend Rudy."

"Really? Well, there you go, Sherlock and Watson! Looks like you just solved that case. Congratulations."

"You don't seem too surprised," asked Lo.

"Why should I be? He tried to kill me," I said and held up my bandaged hand.

"Apparently Michelle Bartley had a relationship with Pays Lee too. Carl might have been jealous, or thought he was protecting her," continued Gomez.

"But why did he kill Rudy?" I asked, playing dumb.

"We think he was just in the wrong place at the wrong time."

I nodded. "That's too bad."

"Well, we thought you'd like to know," said Gomez.

"Thanks. So, I guess this means I can get my guns back now?"

"Yeah, you can come by the station house. I'll write up a release," offered Gomez.

"You guys are full of surprises today." I smiled.

Lo and Gomez exchanged looks as I poured the coffees. I

took a sip, and Lo asked, "What about Ernesto Swanzy?"

I thought they were watching me for a tell at the mention of his name, but I didn't let on at all. I simply responded by asking, "Who?"

Gomez placed the mug shot of Swanzy down in front of me and repeated, "Ernesto Swanzy. Remember?"

"Oh, yeah," I said studying the photo. "You still looking for him?"

"We just want to have a little talk with him. Heard he was seen around the building here a few days back," said Gomez.

"Here? News to me," I said picking up the photo again. "What's he got to do with anything?"

"Maybe nothing. Maybe everything. You see him, give us a call." Gomez tossed his card on the counter next to Swanzy's photo. He and Lo exchanged looks, and Gomez nodded toward the door.

As they headed out, I asked, "Don't you guys want your coffee?"

"I'll take a rain check," said Gomez.

"I ain't drinking your coffee. You're the Angel of Death," replied Lo.

I smiled as they went out the door.

I decided I needed to get on with my life, so I wrapped my bandaged hand up in a plastic bag, showered, went out, and bought a new phone. Luckily, I had the insurance so it only cost me the one-hundred-dollar deductible that they'd bill me for. I downloaded all my contacts and settings from the cloud, and as soon as I got back to the Suburban, I called Molly's phone. I got the same disconnect message. I didn't *really* expect anything different, but I still hoped.

When I got back to my place I started in earnest calling around, trying to dig up some work. Without that cash, I was dead broke. After a few initial calls to transportation captains I knew who either wouldn't answer the phone or rudely told me they didn't have anything available, I called Chris DeLuca.

Chris was sympathetic and straight with me. He told me word was out that I was persona non grata. Jimmy Sheehan had made it a personal vendetta to use everything in his power to keep me from being employed. Apparently it was working.

"Hey, Chris, let me ask you. Have you seen Molly in the last couple of days?" I had to ask.

"Are you kidding? You run off with her and then you lose her? What the hell's the matter with you?"

Exactly what I was wondering myself, I told him. I thanked Chris for being upfront and asked him to call me if he heard of anything at all he could throw my way. He told me he would and hung up. I decided to call Jimmy directly, figuring I had nothing to lose at that point, give him a piece of my mind. But of course, he didn't pick up. I thought of leaving him a message, telling him what I really thought of him, but then thought better of it and hung up.

By this point, I was despondent and at a complete loss as to what to do. My thoughts drifted to Jonathan Pichter and how he was able to walk away from all that happened without a shred of remorse or evidence against him. Then it came to me—*Moby Dick*! I dialed Bigsby's number as I went to my bookshelf. Time to use my insurance policy. Bigsby picked up after one ring.

"Mister Millek, I must advise you not to contact this number or my client's number ever again. Is that understood?"

"Hold on, Bigsby. I think I've been very helpful to your client."

"Which is why he's willing to forget about the compensation you've already collected," he said.

"The compensation is gone."

"That is not our problem."

I pulled *Moby Dick* off the shelf and said, "Look, I've got something your client might be interested in."

But when I opened the book, the thumb drive was gone.

"Do you now? And what, Mister Millek, could that be?" Bigsby knew. He knew the thumb drive was gone.

"Bastards…" I said at a loss.

I listened as Bigsby said again, "As I advised you, please do not contact this number or my client ever again. Good day, Mister Millek." And with that he hung up.

CHAPTER 24

The next day, I went to Santa Monica police headquarters. Gomez was true to his word and had cleared the way for me to pick up all my guns. I took them directly to my friend Charlie Hutchins' place. Charlie was a movie armorer and worked out of his home as a gunsmith. He also had a federal firearms license so he could act as a gun dealer as well. He didn't keep any sales inventory on hand but was always buying and selling firearms for what he needed on film shoots. He also brokered sales between private, law-abiding citizens and performed background checks for a fee. I needed some fast cash, and he fronted me five hundred against the sale of my competition Colt .45. It was the one piece he knew he could sell quickly for a good price. He offered to list what others I was willing to part with but I'd have to wait until the sale went through for me to collect anything. I was happy to get the five hundred and headed home.

The next couple of weeks were spent trying to dig up any cash I could in order to survive. I was doing odd boat jobs around the marina—not easy with my hand still on the mend— and selling anything I had that I thought might have some value. Charlie Hutchins sold off most of what I wanted or needed to sell, but I had to wait for background checks to clear from the buyers before I could collect. I was barely able to keep the bill collectors at bay and had to beg Liz Blanco to let me pay off my rent on a weekly basis until I got caught up.

I finally had to make a decision on either selling the Suburban or selling *Stella* to save on the slip fees and stay afloat for a few months. Since I was going to need the Suburban for transportation and any possible work, I called Corey, my buddy the yacht broker, and put *Stella* on the market again.

I continued to spend my days hustling cash any way I could to keep my head above water, using whatever free time I had working on *Stella,* cleaning her up for a good showing. I tried my best to put Molly out of my head while I worked, but now everything aboard *Stella* reminded me of the time we spent together and what we went through. Every time it started to piss me off how Molly just up and left, I had to remember that she was probably better off for doing so. I had dragged her into a dark mess that she didn't deserve. I didn't even care about the money anymore. It hurt like hell that she was gone and made me feel like a fool for getting hurt. I had sworn I was never going to let a woman hurt me like that again after Sandy. I was hoping *Stella* would sell fast so I wouldn't have to be reminded of Molly any longer.

I spent my evenings drinking way more than I should have been in my state of mind. I knew it wasn't doing me any good, but I had to numb the pain. One night, while surfing the web, perusing the trades for work, I came across an article and review of "the release of the late Michelle Bartley's final recordings before her untimely death. Produced by the late Pays Lee." It looked like Pichter released the master recordings and made a record deal. I couldn't believe how he was going to cash in and capitalize on not only his wife's death but Pays Lee's as well. Jonathan Pichter sure knew how to play all the aces.

As a last-ditch effort, I Googled Gabriella Vassey to see what she was up to and if I could hit her up for some work. I came across an article in *The Hollywood Reporter* that Gabby was producing a film through her studio production deal. I sat up when I saw that Jonathan Pichter was mentioned in the same article for discovering a promising young screenwriter and director named Al Phillips. It appeared Pichter had brokered a seven-figure deal on Philips' first screenplay and directorial debut with Gabby's production company. This was all like rubbing salt in my wounds. It was as if Pichter were speaking directly to me, letting me know he got my Al Phillips thumb drive with the copies I made of Lauren's illicit photos. The icing on the cake was Phillips' first picture was scheduled to start shooting the following month in Maui. Landing the leading female role was newcomer Yael Idelson, "the sexy, young, up-and-coming Israeli super-model." There was a photo of her and Al Phillips together at some Hollywood red carpet event. I was dumbfounded. I'd like to say I couldn't believe it, but as I said before, I've learned to believe anything is possible in Hollywood.

As for Lauren, at least Pichter kept her out of the limelight. Out of curiosity, I did an online search for her. All I found were some innocent Crosswind Academy social media pages of Lauren making the debate team, singing in the school glee club, and multiple offerings of condolences on the death of her mother. I wanted to believe she was living life as a normal yet upscale teenager, but I had to wonder what control Pichter had over her public image. I really hoped she would turn out all right, but with her history, and living under Pichter's reign, I had my doubts. Would she ever find out it was her stepfather that had her mother killed? Would she learn that the man who sexually abused her was actually her biological father? Who knows? Only in Hollywood.

The next day, Corey called to say he had made an appointment with a potential buyer. This time it was someone looking for an ocean cruiser and not some Southern California bikini bucket. So here I was once again, waiting to take a potential buyer out on a test sail. And once again, I sat and waited, and I started contemplating how I had arrived at this low point in my life. And once again, they were late, so I went below and put on a pot of coffee. The pot was beginning to boil when I heard Corey's voice call out.

"Ahoy, Captain Mikey, you in there?"

"Aye aye," I muttered and popped up out of the companionway to greet Corey.

Corey turned to introduce me to the buyer, and I froze, dumbstruck. Standing there, with her strawberry blond locks waving in the breeze, tanned, freckled, wearing a striped French sailor's blouse, smiling as she removed her designer sunglasses, and looking more beautiful than ever...was Molly.

"Mike, this is Molly. Molly, this is Captain Mike. He'll be showing you around and if you like what you see, taking you for a test sail," said Corey in broker mode, helping Molly aboard. She carried a large canvas boat tote over her shoulder.

Corey continued, "Molly's looking to cruise the South Pacific and beyond. I told you had just the boat for her."

Molly! I couldn't believe my eyes. And I couldn't utter a word.

"Now, if you excuse me, I've got to run back to my office, but when I get back, if you like what you see, we'll take her for a spin," Corey explained, looking to me for back up. I was dumbfounded and couldn't say a thing as I stared at Molly.

It was Molly who responded, her eyes on mine. "I'm sure Captain Mike can take me out for a test sail."

"Sure, if you're okay with that. Mike will take good care of you." Corey looked to me for confirmation, but I kept my eyes locked on Molly's. "When you get back, swing by the office if you want to discuss terms. Or if you want to see something else," he said to Molly.

Corey looked to me again, winked, and waved as he went back down the dock toward his pickup truck.

"She's a beauty." Molly climbed down the companionway into the cabin.

"Yes, she is," as I continued to stare at Molly. "Look, I have to apologize. I've decided the boat's not for sale. You see I promised someone an ocean cruise that I haven't delivered on yet."

Molly looked at me quizzically.

"That's too bad. I brought cash."

She swung the tote off her shoulder and unzipped it to show me the money, still neatly bound and tightly stuffed inside.

I tossed the bag aside and stepped up closer to her. We gazed into each other's eyes. I was looking for a sign wondering where we stood, with each other. Her eyes brightened as she smiled. She reached down, took my hand and led me forward to the V-berth.

"Request permission to have an audience with the captain," she said.

I smiled, following her. "Permission granted."

"We've got some catching up to do," she said.

"Yes, we do."

ACKNOWLEDGMENTS

I would like to acknowledge and thank my editor, the late Peggy Hagemen who I am deeply sorry to say recently lost her battle to cancer, for all her help, insight, and guidance with this book. Though we never actually met in person, she treated me with professionalism like a long-time colleague and with the warmness of a friend. Based on the tributes I've read about her, I know she had the love and respect of many and will be sorely missed.

I want to acknowledge and thank Elizabeth Vialle Jankowski for being the best ex-wife a guy could ever have. She will always be family to me. I would like to thank my old boss, dear friend, and much more, Rupert Holmes, author, playwright, singer-songwriter, for being the nicest guy in show business and for his gracious words of encouragement. I would also like to acknowledge and thank Eric Campbell and Lance Wright at Down & Out Books for their support, author and film editor Lawrence Maddox, and two of my oldest and closest friends, Rob Andriani and Mike Mariconda who have always stuck with me through thick and thin.

And I also want to acknowledge all the men and women I've had the pleasure of working with over the years in the entertainment business that have shared the comradery, the laughs, the good times, and all the trials and tribulations, much of which has been an inspiration for this book. I particularly want to acknowledge and give my utmost thanks to my screenwriting partner, film and television director, and award-winning author, John Shepphird for his constant support and encouragement, his perpetual inspiration, his knowledgeable advice, his keen and always insightful feedback, his simpatico sense of humor, and most of all for his never-ending and unwavering friendship.

STEVEN JANKOWSKI was born and raised in The Bronx, NY and spent most of his adult life hustling a living in the entertainment business. He spent the first ten years out of high school working as a stagehand in the 1970's NYC Rock & Roll music scene, and on the road as a band roadie and road manager. In the mid-80's he returned to school to study film at Hunter College, and then moved to Los Angeles to earn his MFA in Screenwriting at USC. Since then Steve has written or co-written over 30 screenplays with nine of them having been produced.

Below the Line marks Steven's first foray into fiction writing and draws from his many years of experience in the film and music industries, as well as his love of sailing. Steven currently resides in the Los Angeles port city of San Pedro, CA.

BOOKS

On the following pages are a few
more great titles from the
Down & Out Books publishing family.

For a complete list of books and to
sign up for our newsletter,
go to DownAndOutBooks.com.

Don't Shoot the Drummer
A Lou Crasher Novel
Jonathan Brown

Down & Out Books
November 2020
978-1-64396-150-7

A security guard is murdered during a home robbery of a house tented for fumigation and Lou Crasher is asked to solve the murder. The rock-drumming amateur P.I. is up for it, because his brother Jake is the one asking. Lou fights to keep his musical day job and catch the killers.

When the bullets fly he hopes all involved respect his golden rule: Don't Shoot The Drummer.

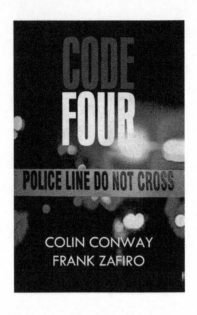

Code Four
A Charlie-316 Crime Novel
Colin Conway and Frank Zafiro

Down & Out Books
November 2020
978-1-64396-157-6

The last two years have been tumultuous ones for the Spokane Police Department. The agency has suffered from scandal and police officer deaths and underneath, a secret and deadly game of cat and mouse has been playing out.

Now the Department of Justice has arrived to determine if federal intervention is needed. This disrupts everyone's agenda and threatens to expose dark secrets, and end careers.

All Due Respect 2020
Chris Rhatigan & David Nemeth, editors

All Due Respect, an imprint of
Down & Out Books
November 2020
978-1-64396-165-1

Twelve short stories from the top writers in crime fiction today.

Featuring the work of Stephen D. Rogers, Tom Leins, Michael Pool, Andrew Davie, Sharon Diane King, Preston Lang, Jay Butkowski, Steven Berry, Craig Francis Coates, Bobby Mathews, Michael Penncavage, and BV Lawson.

White Trash and Dirty Dingoes
Jason Parent

Shotgun Honey, an imprint of
Down & Out Books
July 2020
978-1-64396-101-9

Gordon thought he'd found the girl of his dreams. But women like Sarah are tough to hang on to.

When she causes the disappearance of a mob boss's priceless Chihuahua, she disappears herself, and the odds Gordon will see his lover again shrivel like nuts in a polar plunge.

With both money and love lost, he's going to have to kill some SOBs to get them back.

Made in the USA
Monee, IL
21 December 2020